The Thousand Dollar Yacht

The Thousand Dollar Yacht

BY ANTHONY BAILEY

Illustrated by Peter Tripp

INTERNATIONAL MARINE PUBLISHING COMPANY
CAMDEN, MAINE

"Haze at Napatree" appeared in somewhat different
form in the October 1967 issue of The Skipper.
"A Week on the Lower Connecticut" appeared
in somewhat different form in the February 1968
issue of Holiday *magazine.*

First published by The Macmillan
Company, New York, 1968. Printed in
paperback by Land & Sea, Stonington,
Connecticut, 1979.

Published in 1988 by
International Marine Publishing Company.
Route 1, P.O. Box 220,
Camden, Maine 04843

Printed and bound by
BookCrafters, Chelsea, Michigan

10 9 8 7 6 5 4 3 2 1

Library of Congress Cataloging-in-Publication Data

Bailey, Anthony.
    The thousand dollar yacht / by Anthony Bailey.
        p.   cm.
    ISBN 0-87742-967-7
    1. Bailey, Anthony. 2. Seamen—United States—Biography.
3. Yachts and yachting.   I. Title.
GV812.5.B34A3   1988
797.1'24'0924—dc19
[B]   88-12267
                                                           CIP

TO

Jonathan Rowe; Selwyn Slater; Wheezy Williams, C. G. Bailey;
the late Commander Hammond, R.N.; Reginald Bennett, M.P.;
George Dore; Uffa Fox; Richard Baron; Rear Admiral P. Gick,
R.N. Ret.; Y. K. Adam; J. McVitty; Paula Chapin; R & R Gutwillig;
Richard Baum; L. R. Hills; J. E. Dodson Sr.; J. E. Dodson Jr.;
John Dodge; David Johnstone; Wm. W. Robinson; Duke Winter;
Winslow Ayer; Wm. B. White; R. McCullough; Donald Robinson;
C. C. Van Zandt; and Margot Bailey

who at one time or another lent me their
boats or took me sailing.

Contents

To go to sea! Why, it is to have the experience of
Noah—to realize the deluge.

> —Thoreau, *Cape Cod.*

The history of seafaring is a part of the study of man, it
has its practical side, field work performed in the pleas-
antest of circumstances, and it is great fun, providing you
don't take it too seriously, as if boats were an art form, or
human beings, or ideas, or God.

> —Basil Greenhill, *Sailing for a Living.*

Foreword

For the person who wrote it, a book sometimes feels like a child, a creature to which one has given life and which then leads a life of its own. Yet whereas a child changes in the course of growing up, and the world around it with the passage of time changes too, a book does not. *The Thousand Dollar Yacht,* twenty years after its first appearance, is still the same batch of words and drawings, with the same title. On the other hand, the times which made one thousand dollars seem a small but in my case just achievable price to pay for a twenty-eight foot boat have altered to an extent where that amount is almost derisory—it would scarcely purchase a new eight-foot dinghy. However, for those who aren't overdependent on capital, inflation is mostly a matter of numbers. The principles that governed the building of the "yacht" remain, and so in warm spaces in my memory do the pleasures associated with the creation of both boat and book.

To touch first on the making of the boat, in 1962 and 1963, some of the pleasures were those of conspicuous thrift, of getting things for next-to-nothing. Such delights may not be closely

linked with late twentieth-century Western civilization, but they
are perhaps more commonly enjoyed by sailors than by those
devoted to other leisure activities or sports. Many sailors are
keen on bargains and on "making do." They end-for-end slightly
worn halyards. They use up paint from old cans. They are
beachcombers, excited by finding a possibly useful bucket or
hunk of timber. They save shackles which have lost their pins,
and pins from lost shackles, and are appropriately thrilled when,
one day, a match is made. And clearly in any time there are going
to be people who—wanting a boat—don't or can't reach for a
credit card or think of calling a marine-mortgage consultant.
Instead, they ponder lifeboats, ships' boats, workboats, which
might be converted and get one agreeably afloat. They consider
the example of earlier yachtsmen like Captain Voss, who made
his epic world-ranging voyage in a modified British Columbian
dugout canoe (whose thirty-eight-foot length included the
figurehead). I came across a newspaper item only a year or so
ago describing a large dory yacht just launched by a doctor in
Maine, and he had accomplished this at roughly twice what it cost
me. So it can still be done, and always will be done, as long as
people have sea-fever and trust their impulse for simplicity, for
the less-than-orthodox, for the craft which has never been mar-
keted or merchandised. And the joys attached may be rightly
described by allusion to other forms of similarly individual creation—the writing of a poem, the painting of a picture, the birth
of a child—though possibly without claiming for one's vessel
significance in the progress of human culture.

Among the good things involved in the building of my yacht,
the *Billy Ruffian,* was association with a number of tremendous
individuals. They are to be encountered in the pages that follow,
but as an example let me mention Wolcott Palmer, whom I met
in the course of my search for cheap mast hoops, and who in his
back-country workshop proudly showed me the homemade
machine, until recently operated by water power, on which he
turned out wooden hoops used in the entrances of lobster pots—

hoops which, at ten cents apiece, served well for my purposes. The boat itself when launched had some novel advantages, not least as a capacious floating playpen; its immense and deep cockpit was hard for small children to fall out of and furnished all sorts of intricate places for them to disport themselves, happily and damply. The *Billy Ruffian* was not a great windward performer, and hadn't been expected to be, but equally unexpected was the enchantment of being at the helm and suddenly aware that this boat made a marvelous sight, creaming along on a broad reach: that this was a unique craft, interesting to look at, and conducive to a unique pride for her owner.

The book was written in 1967, partly in the attic study of our Stonington, Connecticut, home, partly during an eastbound transatlantic voyage of the liner *France* (those were the last great days of sea travel, when passage on a liner cost little more than a plane ticket), and partly in my parents' house in England. It was written very much as a personal record, out of personal enthusiasm. But after publication it soon was seen to have more general byproducts. Many letters arrived from people interested in doing something similar. There were phone calls from what to me were out-of-the-way places—from Alaska, from Alabama, and from Los Angeles, where a man in an airport callbox used up half an hour between planes quizzing me, for example, about how my experiment with ex-utility pole rigging wire had worked out. And there was one communication that made me feel particularly apologetic. This was a letter from the man who had owned the Seagull outboard which I had bought for twenty-five dollars on retrieval from the bottom of a Fishers Island harbor. In writing about this, perhaps to accentuate the bargain, I had made this gentleman sound like a ritzy yachtsman, but he turned out to be the owner of a simple enough craft, with instincts remarkably like my own, and his good-humored letter pointed this out with very little in the way of injured feelings.

The big dory turned out to have one serious disadvantage. This was that she was hard to leave behind when we made summer trips back to family in England or I took long research jaunts for new writing projects. The *Billy Ruffian* wasn't the sort of boat one could easily charter or even lend to friends, who might not take to her idiosyncrasies. On the other hand, one didn't want to leave her out of the water, parching in summer sun, while we enjoyed a wet August in Sussex or moved from house to flat to boat in the crowded Netherlands. Thus, eventually and regretfully, I sold the thousand dollar yacht (for fifteen hundred) and bought a slightly more conventional sloop, simpler to lend in return for some help with her upkeep.

The man who bought the *Billy Ruffian* was a marine artist, perhaps seduced by her blue sails and sweeping sheer. I lost sight of her for a few years and when I saw her again, she had a figurehead, ratlines, and deadeyes, and had been renamed something like "Itinerant"—all of which hurt. Then, later still, there were reports that she had been glimpsed looking neglected somewhere up the Connecticut River. But, several years on, our phone rang one day in Stonington and a voice asked if I'd care to come down to the dock to cast an eye on my former craft. There was the *Billy Ruffian* looking spruce again. A young couple were aboard, and evidently having a good time in her. "Where are you headed?" I asked. "The Bahamas," they cheerfully replied. *The Bahamas!* Well, I said, choosing my words carefully for fear of seeming an awful wet blanket, you might want to stay inshore, in protected waters, indeed in the inland waterway, as long as possible. However, good luck. Godspeed. *Bon voyage.*

I sometimes wonder if they got there, or where they got to. Yet we all have Bahamas of one sort or other as a goal at some point in our lives, and are fortunate if we find the right boats in which to sail to them. I'm glad that the *Billy Ruffian* took me to Bahamas of my own, local but bountiful, and that in this new edition of *The Thousand Dollar Yacht*, the *Billy Ruffian* sails to them once again.

* * *

My thanks must be recorded: to the late Peter Ritner, to Rose-mary Wallace Gutwillig, and to Jonathan Eaton, who at different times saw this book into print. And I thank most especially Peter Tripp, without whom neither boat nor book would have taken shape as they did, and whose splendid drawings continue, I think, to catch the excitement and the impromptu spirit of our enterprise.

Tony Bailey
Greenwich
January 1988

1

Hunting

In my part of New England there is a saying that some of the best deals are those you do not make. There is no doubt in my mind that some of the best boats are those which, fortunately, you manage not to buy. My neighbor Peter Tripp and I drove down to City Island one gray November day to look over a bargain I had heard about: a twenty-three–foot centerboard sloop with dacron sails and auxiliary engine for

something less than six hundred dollars. City Island is a down-at-heel offshoot of the Bronx, an island overlaid with a grid-iron pattern of streets on which the houses and shops are shabby and the boatyards and yacht clubs at the water-ends of them suggest that thirty years have passed since their better days. It was snowing by the time we got there. But Peter and I crawled about the boat, which we found in one of the shabbiest boatyards. It was a tubby little vessel, with no cabin furnishings, a few boards lying loose instead of a floor or sole, a rusty Palmer eight-horse engine, a disconnected water closet, a mast that looked as if it had been inherited from a sailing dinghy, and below the waterline, stem to stern, do-it-yourself fiberglass sheathing that covered God knows what sick fastenings, soggy planks, and creeping rot. In some places the fiberglass was cracked and peeling. The boat's transom was almost the width of her maximum beam. Her underwater shape was that of an old-fashioned claw-legged bathtub. Yet within, with bare ribs and planking the only décor, she seemed to have a great deal of room. I went and stood for a while in the wet, falling snow on the far side of the marine railway, from which I could see the whole boat without turning my head. In my mind I added a bowsprit, a bumpkin, gaff rig, a painted sheer strake, and at four hundred dollars—the price I decided I would offer for her—I didn't see how I could go wrong. But, home again, the enchantment slipped a little. I thought about it for several weeks, went to see her again, and finally called the owner, whose rather desperate advertisement had been appearing daily in the *New York Times*. He was difficult to reach. At last he called, from a hospital somewhere in the Bronx. His wife, he said, had just had a baby; it was his reason for selling the boat. I felt happy that I was going to be able to help him out in this hour of need. I asked about the baby. I mentioned the boat and the sum of four hundred dollars, and wondered for an instant why he sounded disappointed, until I took in the fact that he was saying that the baby was a boy and that he had sold the boat that afternoon for three hundred and fifty.

From a distance of half a dozen years I am not sorry I failed to acquire that bargain, or any of the other boats I nearly bought during the same period. One of the notable facts about boat-hunting is that it is perfectly possible to develop a liking, and sometimes even a sort of love, for at least half the craft one examines. The old comparison of women and boats remains just. Indeed, a man in dire need of a boat can be quite as hungry and as uncertain of his true taste as a man lacking a woman.

I spent a pleasant day in Massachusetts—part of it in Westport, at the mouth of the pretty river there, where I came across a Wianno Senior for sale quite cheaply. The asking price was twelve hundred, the yard manager told me, but he thought the owner might go a bit lower. I thought seriously about her, although the two bunks were cramped and there wasn't even sitting headroom; it was like lowering yourself into a cocoon. There was also talk of a little rot in the garboards. Apart from that, she was an attractive, dignified yacht. The yard manager said, "JFK owns one, you know." In Mystic a few weeks later I considered a venerable British cutter, with plumb stem, uncharacteristic shoal draft, rather bumpy planking, and a fine upstanding coachroof, reminiscent of a hansom cab in the days when Sherlock Holmes took them from Baker Street—there was, in fact, a scent of fog and Channel weather about her. Elsewhere I missed a Folkboat by a week—the anxious owner, moving to Idaho, let her go for fourteen hundred—and I was nearly talked into buying a converted Star. In Westbrook, Connecticut, I found a different kind of boat, a 26-foot converted lifeboat named, with fidelity, *Nightmare*. To reach her I had to drive past several rows of shabby shore cottages to a marina, where no one knew much about her except that her owners, two young men from Hartford, occasionally came there to buy gas for their outboard. *Nightmare* was moored in a nearby creek. It was hard to say whether she was carvel- or clinker-planked. She was half full of water and nearly capsized when I stepped aboard. I noted that the water tasted strongly of salt, that most of the room was occupied by the original rowing thwarts, which presumably still held her together, and that an eel was swimming in the outboard well. I climbed back onto the bank of the creek. The effect of the surroundings—calm water, grass growing to the edge of the bank, swallows darting across the field, and the summer houses silhouetted against the horizon —conspired to give *Nightmare* a romantic quality. I thought I could patch her up and spend some pleasant hours on her amid these marshes.

So there is a sense in which every boat is the boat one might buy. They all have "possibilities." And they all generally have a drawback, which may be price, or rot, or not in the end quite stacking up against one's optimistic criteria. Most sailors have in their minds the ideal specifications for a boat: fast, seaworthy, beautiful, spacious, and cheap. One needs to do a great deal of looking at boats, sitting in them on their cradles in falling snow, poking with an ice pick into butt blocks and rib ends, shining a flashlight into murky, oil-clogged recesses, and taking measurements with a tape held in frozen fingers, before one can begin to make up one's mind —partly from impatience, partly from experience—where in the inevitable compromise the weight must fall. One needs to loaf around boatyard offices and shops and sit gossiping in the store of a place like Dodson's, in Stonington, with the coffee percolator light glowing red and the lid of the doughnut box wide open. I say "one needs," though there's little pain in the necessity. "Why don't you buy the *Scarlet Rover?*" said Johnny Dodson one winter afternoon, and immediately a chorus of voices began to tell how the *Scarlet Rover* won her class in Fall Off-Soundings Regatta three—or was it four? —years ago when two boats were dismasted, one sank, and waterspouts chased class B-1 all the way from Cerberus Shoal to Valiant Rock. *Scarlet Rover's* owner took good care of his ship; in fact, he had relays of high school boys pumping her out daily during the summer vacation. Moreover, the ship took good care of him. Last season, coming back from the Vineyard single-handed, he went below to use the separately compartmented head. While he was doing so, the *Scarlet Rover* lurched, causing the drawers to fall out of the chest of drawers built opposite the head door, jamming the door shut. The trapped owner banged, pushed, kicked, and finally, it seems, yelled to no avail, until—after five hours, in which she sailed on perfectly happy without him—the *Scarlet Rover* came about from port to starboard tack, heeled the other way, and all the drawers fell back into place.

"How much is he asking?"

"He's talking five, but he'll take two and a half."

One sage piece of boating lore proposes that the time to buy a yacht is at the end of the season, when the cost of hauling and of winter storage supposedly have a sodium pentothal or truth serum-like effect on the owner, lowering his boat's price. In fact, boat owners who are untrustworthy in the fall become even more so in the spring, when in hope of being able to unload the old bucket before another season's pumping is upon them, they will camouflage with a glossy coat of paint her brittle chainplates, cracked horn timber, and rotten planking. On just such a freshly done-up svelte thirty-two–foot yawl I nearly made a down-payment saved up for a house. The yawl had "passed survey a year before." She needed new rigging, but for a boat of her size and character the price was reasonable. I thought about it. Fortunately, a more impetuous customer rushed in and paid the full price. He took delivery in the water and soon discovered twelve frames needed replacing, her entire bottom required replanking, and the whole yacht had to be refastened—four thousand dollars worth.

New boats caused me less worry. To begin with, those chrome and plastic parcels of industrial design that were propped up in the Coliseum at Boat Show time were always far out of reach. Base price $9862. Optional extras, such as sails, rigging, head, mattresses, stove, and life jackets, not to speak of such necessary items as pulpit, winches, St. Christopher's medal, and sales tax, bring you rather quickly to a plateau of $16,989, with the summit still nowhere in sight.* A much more tolerable and less physically exhausting form of boat-hunting can be conducted with feet up and beer in hand, while surveying yacht designs in books, magazines, or brokers' circulars. In the course of five years of metropolitan apartment existence, I amassed several filing drawers of replies from yacht brokers, designers, and builders in half a dozen countries, thanking me for my interest and enclosing brochures, photographs, construction details, and occasionally large-scale cutaway drawings of the craft for which they anticipated I would place an order "at my earliest convenience." Naval architects, one felt, must be very patient men, with numerous secretaries. By these means I became enamored of a small Dutch steel sloop, a Norwegian fisherman-type pine-planked motor-sailer, and an English four-ton fiberglass cutter. I placed an advertisement in the monthly *National and Maine Coast Fisherman,* asking for a cheap, ungadgety sailing boat. In reply I got details of sharpie ketches and converted whaleboats. I wrote to Glasgow for an illustrated report of a competition for a thousand pound (i.e., $2800) yacht and found the yachts interesting, though none of the attractive ones could be built for less than $4500. Many eve-

---

* I have never, in any event, found the heavily hot dog scented air and foot-tiring floors of boat shows at all conducive to the purchase of a boat. However, my friend Yaacov, who appears later in these pages, has told me of fabulous bargains that can be arranged with near-bankrupt builders on the last day of such shows, when exhibited boats can be acquired for a token payment to the dealer and the promise to deal with and pay off the representatives of the fifteen unions required to move the boat out of the show building.

nings after dinner, instead of watching *Naked City* or reading Thoreau, I pored over designs in yachting magazines.
There is a special gaze, a sort of hypnotized stare, that
men develop as they look at the sail plan or line drawing
of a possible boat. It isn't really an examination or analy-
sis, but is more a giving-up of the beholder to the object
beheld—a semimystical act, producing little that is concrete
and especially annoying to people like wives, who speak to
you and receive no answer. Sometimes I had moments of
guilt. Was this all a waste of time? How serious could a man
become about boats and still function and succeed in every-
day society? I took comfort in the notion that, in an age in
which leisure was rapidly overtaking work as man's principal
preoccupation, boats had a redeeming quality. I was happy to
read in a work by David Jones that James Joyce had once
said to Oliver St. John Gogarty, "Practical life or 'art' com-
prehends all our activities, from boat building to poetry."
Loren Eiseley gave me support when he wrote that human
beings were nine-tenths seawater. I was obeying the call of
the brine in my blood. I was going back to the sea. In any
event, I now have pleasant memories of those city dream
ships, of *Vivette,* a lovely, long East Anglian yawl, and *Lemster*, a stubby steel sloop. I have a sense of having had real
adventures in them, finding *Vivette* a misery to get out of
Harwich harbor one foggy morning and *Lemster* rather noisy
in the short steep seas of the Ijsselmeer.

When I moved from New York to Stonington, it was in
some ways a return to a childhood landscape. Stonington
lacks the more extreme tides and the wide mudflats of Portchester, a village at the head of Portsmouth harbor, in southern England. However, it has the same accessibility to marine
things and the same quality of being historic without any
denial of the importance of the present. In Portchester, the
past was simply close at hand. Overshadowing Portchester
Creek was a castle, built of chalky stone—it had Roman foun-

dations, Saxon walls, and a Norman keep. English kings had
sailed from it for France, and French prisoners had been
incarcerated there—their names were carved on the inner
walls. From the top of the keep one could see Portsmouth
dockyard and the spars of Nelson's flagship *Victory*, enshrined
there. At low tide, a narrow stretch of gray water snaked
northeast from the moored ammunition hulks and moth-
balled minesweepers, a channel running between tall pilings

on the edge of wide expanses of mud. It ran across the danger area of Tipner rifle range, where it bent a little to the west. Then at Basket Point Shoal it turned north again in a channel that narrowed between Horsea Island, with its torpedo-testing establishment, and the Castle, and finally it turned right and dried out in Paulsgrove Lake at the foot of Portsdown Hill. This was the Creek. I could see a small slice of it from my bedroom window, on the third floor of the converted barn and cottage we lived in on Castle Street.

Stonington is a little more off the beaten-track. The New Haven shore line goes by the village, but passenger trains rarely stop. Natives ask newcomers a trifle jealously, "How did you find Stonington?" There's no response guaranteed to please. Attempting to answer the question, I have referred to weekend visits, to a voyage in a Block Island Race on a yawl that developed a leak in the stuffing box and took refuge in Stonington, the nearest port, and to friends who went off to the sunny Adriatic for the winter and left us in charge of their Stonington house. One way or another, we became acquainted with the place and (gathering a little steam now) found that it was not only pretty but a marvelous place to live. Its inhabitants the best sort of New Englanders—not at all like old England—a rather Victorian atmosphere—altogether a miraculous stroke of fortune that it exists—and so forth. That may do.

In fact, Stonington isn't particularly quaint and so far it isn't too prettified. The fishing fleet survives on a modest scale, trash-fishing. The lobstermen seem to thrive. There is a velvet mill and a factory that makes plastic squeegee bottles. There is a percentage—not overwhelming, but sufficient to make happy the merchants of the town—of prosperous summer people. There is a smaller percentage of New York intelligentsia, who move up, and sometimes stay—they become Stonington intelligentsia. Like Portchester, with a major port close by, Stonington is the home of many active and retired naval officers. Indeed, the crucial moment in its otherwise uneventful history came in August 1814, when a small British squadron under Nelson's former aide, Captain Thomas Hardy, anchored off the town for a day or so and let fly several salvoes. The British believed that the natives of Stonington were manufacturing torpedoes and other infernal devices for use against the blockading fleet. (In fact, at Norwich the natives were.) The Stonington defenders fired several rounds in reply, perhaps damaging the British morale more than their vessels, and Captain Hardy withdrew—the word senior officers prefer to retreat.

Not long after moving to Stonington I met Peter Tripp, a tall, bearlike man with a jutting chin and a cautious way when walking of putting one foot down slowly in front of the other, as if he isn't quite sure the ground is going to be there. (On boats, Peter always goes barefooted.) Peter was an old hand at boat-dreaming, and with Ringnes beer, pen and scratch pad at hand, he provided spoken and drawn ac companiment for some of my considerations at this time. His own predilection just then was for five-masted schooners of the kind he'd seen as a child off Rye, in Western Long Island Sound. A graduate of Yale, he had served as a wartime naval officer on LSTs, as a mate on a cargo ship, a deckhand on tugs, a draftsman in the Brooklyn Navy Yard, and a pipefitter at Electric Boat Company. He had owned a small gaff sloop and later a fiberglass Triton, on which he lived summer and winter in Stonington harbor, until she burned one Sunday morning while he was in church. Peter was an obstinate romantic whose preference plainly was for boats that carried cargoes, such as coal or seed oysters, but after the loss of his Triton he decided to think small. On a trip to Maine he came across a pretty Whitehall rowing boat, finely built with a wine-glass stern. He bought it and had it brought down by pickup truck, but he didn't keep it for long; he couldn't afford to. On its arrival in Stonington, the boat was observed by several

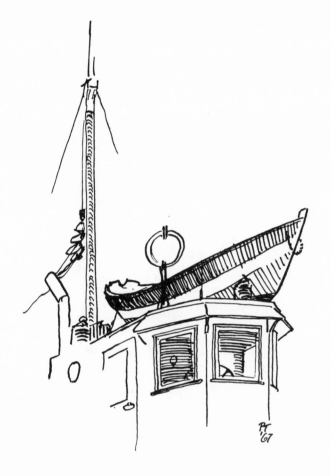

boat-minded people, and inquiries and offers were made at once. When the offers got to twice the price Peter had paid for it, he was unable to hold out. "Done!" he said. Then, without a boat again, he decided the time had come to find out about a kind of vessel he had long been interested in, and whose perky shapes he had admired on the pilot-house roofs of Stonington fishing draggers. Peter went to Captain Jacobs who ran a ship's chandler's store on Longo's Dock and ordered one—a standard fifteen-foot dory built by Hiram Lowell, in Amesbury, Massachusetts.

2

The Right Heading

One morning in early fall a well-dressed man came into Dodson Boatyard and said he would like to trade in his old outboard for a new one. Johnny Dodson, the son of the owner, told him that they didn't take trade-ins, but they would be happy to sell him a new motor and try to find him a buyer for his old one, which happened to be a Seagull Century-plus long shaft with clutch and which also happened to have been dropped off the stern of a yacht in West Harbor, Fishers Island. The outboard had failed to start on re-emergence a day and a half later from those ritzy depths. Johnny, a long, hound-dog sort of individual, called me. He said that he knew I didn't own an appropriate boat, but that an engine was something I'd undoubtedly need sooner or later. The Seagull, he reminded me, was a British job, a low-powered, high-thrust, simply made machine, labeled The Best Outboard for the World. Despite this Rolls-Royce touch, it was more like a Model A. Who knew, this drowned motor might even be a bargain? So on the following day we sailed over to West Harbor in the *White Wing,* Johnny's forty-four-year-old Alden schooner, in order to meet the owner of the outboard and inspect it. Johnny had assured me that a couple of days underwater would be as bad for a Seagull as for a fish. But now, on shore, I heard him muttering about corrosion, electrolysis, magnetoes, and the state—which sounded dire enough—of being frozen-up. It seemed the right moment for me to say that twenty-five dollars was all I could afford. The owner gave us a doubtful look but he said "Okay," and the motor was mine. On the way back to Stonington, Johnny said that it actually might need a new magneto. However, that weekend we had staying with us an old friend, Yaacov Adam, formerly of the Free French, British, and Israeli navies, who had been in a Moscow prison and at a California university where he had studied refrigerator engineering. Yaacov plays a larger part in this story later on, but I will say for now that he is a whiz at acquiring and mending things; he thrives in a world of conspicuous, wasteful consumption. In the boatyard machine shop Yaacov cleaned the engine: he applied carbon tet and compressed air to dry it; he took a wire brush to the ignition and carburetor systems, and he adjusted the spark-plug gap. We drained and refilled the gas tank with the right mixture of gas and oil. Then we placed the engine on the testing barrel, and on the third pull of the starting cord it went.

I had my auxiliary engine; now for the boat.

That October I went out quite often with Peter in his new dory, which was painted bright orange-red. He kept it at the top of a ramp by the Sea Village Restaurant, on the east side of Stonington Point, and pulled it in and out on wooden rollers. His equipment comprised two sets of unpainted oars and tholepins, which are pegs to lock the oar in place on the gunwale. He bought a small dory sail for six dollars on South Street, in Manhattan, and two closet poles for mast and sprit from the Stonington lumber yard. On bright October after-

noons with little breeze we rowed the dory to windward; then,
after sufficient exercise, sailed home downwind, using an oar
to steer with and the smoke from Peter's cigar for a wind
vane. It amazed us how nippily that fifteen-foot dory moved
along under her thirty-five square feet of porous muslin sail
and the weight of two large men. Of course, this was broad-
reaching and running before the wind. But one afternoon
when I was at the steering oar, I asked Peter to sit a few inches
to leeward, which immediately gave us a perilous angle of
heel. Then I hauled in the pajama-cord mainsheet, trimming
the sail, and attempted to make the dory sail into the wind.
We were in the narrows between the north end of Sandy
Point and the peninsula of Salt Acres. To get back to Stonington we had to tack, and tack we did, half a dozen times where
an ordinary sailing boat might have tacked twice. We sailed
about seventy-five degrees off the wind, where most modern
bermuda-rigged boats sail at forty-five degrees. We had no

keel to give us an effective grip on the water, but heeled over, with her lee chine dug in, the dory definitely made more to windward than she lost through sliding off to leeward. We decided that a dory with a centerboard and a better-cut sail would go upwind quite well.

It wasn't long before I began to think about the dory as a yacht. A dory is cheap. It has a bottom made of flat boards, which can be easily sprung into a fore and aft curve. It is usually planked with flat though flaring sides, the sheer of the boat taking its form from the fact that the boards are all the same width and not specially shaped as in most boats. The fact that it is easy to build reduces labor costs. Furthermore, the dory has a long seagoing history, and it generally follows that any implement or device that stays in use over several centuries has a number of good qualities to recommend it.

As for pedigree, the dory appears to be of French descent. Dory certainly sounds like a French word, and the boats have a lot in common with the Provençal *bêtes*, which are seen in the paintings of Van Gogh—they were rigged with a single lateen sail. The dory may have made the crossing from the old world to the new at first on the deck of Breton and Portuguese schooners, and it was as a ship's boat, which could be mass-produced and carried in quantities on deck, with one dory nested inside another, that the type gained favor on the North American coast. When the schooner reached the Grand Banks the dories were put overboard with a fisherman in each, with a baited long-line. During the course of the day as the dories were loaded with cod and halibut, they became less cranky and more seaworthy. American beach dories were generally rigged with spritsail, jib, and centerboard, although two-masted dories were popular with Italian fishermen in Boston in the 1890's. Indeed, dories have made long sea passages. It was in such a boat that the Gloucester fisherman Howard Blackburn was parted from his schooner in a winter gale in the Gulf of Maine. His dory-mate died of exposure, but Blackburn froze his hands to the oars and rowed to shore. Thereafter, with fingers amputated, he built several boats and made a transatlantic passage in one. Before Blackburn, another New England fisherman named Alfred Johnson had sailed the Atlantic in forty-six days in a twenty-foot dory, *Centennial.* Captain and Mrs. Crapo sailed the same ocean in forty-five days a few years later in an improved, ketch-rigged dory, the *New Bedford.* In 1966 four men in two different boats attempted to row across the Atlantic. One crew made it, and their craft was a 20-foot Yorkshire dory.

One of the greatest dory men of all was Captain Joshua Slocum. His most publicized voyage took place in the *Spray,* the large and roomy converted oyster sloop he sailed alone around the world—the first person to do so. But in the 1880's, while master of a cargo vessel, Captain Joshua and his family were shipwrecked in the River Plate. Having no funds and quite literally stranded, the captain and a party of Uruguayans built on the river shore a 35-foot sampan-rigged dory, *Liberdade,* using shipwrecked materials and native woods. For tools they had "an axe, an adze, two saws, one half-inch auger, one six-eighths and one three-eighths auger bit; two large sail needles, which we converted into nailing bits; one roper, that answered for a punch; and, most precious of all, a file that we found in an old sail-bag washed up on the beach." Then they set out to sail home from Montevideo. They found the *Liberdade* sailed fast and well, and the most dangerous experience they had on the trip to Washington, D.C.—the destination the captain chose with a rather faulty sense of publicity—was when, after a gale had blitzed their sails, they accepted a tow into Rio de Janeiro from the mail steamer *Finance,* commanded by Captain Baker, an old friend. While Mrs. Slocum and young Garfield, the younger son, took passage on the steamer, Captain Slocum and his oldest son Victor conned the big dory. The towing hawser had been made fast.

" 'Look out,' said Baker, as the steamer began to move ahead, 'look out that I don't snake that canoe out from under you.'

'Go on with your mails, Baker,' was all I could say, 'don't blow up your ship with my wife and son on board, and I will look out for the packet on the other end of the rope.'

"Baker opened her up to thirteen knots, but the *Liberdade* held on!"

The danger at that speed, at the end of ninety fathoms of one and a half inch diameter line, was that the *Liberdade* would suddenly sheer off to one side and be towed under. For twenty hours the captain sat at the helm holding her straight on course. Victor was stationed forward, ready with an axe to chop the towline if the *Liberdade* began to sheer. The worst hours came in rough water, when Captain Baker ordered oil to be poured from the steamer's stern in order to make the wake smooth and give the dory calmer sailing. By the time they reached Rio, the great captain had swallowed (he said) "enough oil to cure any amount of consumption." It was also the most thrilling boat-ride of his life, though he wished at the time he hadn't accepted the invitation. Once he had done so, he couldn't back out. "I was bound not to cut the rope that towed us so well; and I knew that Baker wouldn't let go, for it was his rope."

It seemed to me that Howard Chapelle, the marine historian, was right to say that "the large dory represents a seaworthy flat-bottomed type that deserves more attention than it has yet had from boat sailors." I knew that the Gloucester yacht designer, Philip Bolger, had created several dory yachts. I liked the way a dory sat on the water, unladen, like a gull. I thought something about twenty-four feet long would be the largest boat I could afford and the smallest a man, woman, and children could comfortably sail in. And so I wrote to several dory builders for quotations. At this moment, moreover, the *National and Maine Coast Fisherman* began a series of articles about the *grandes doris* of the two French islands, St. Pierre and Miquelon, off Newfoundland. St. Pierre had been a center of rum-running activities during prohibition in America. I also remembered its postage stamps, showing the *grandes doris,* from my childhood stamp-collecting days. John Gardner, technical editor of the *Fisherman,* reported that the St. Pierre fishermen took these craft some twenty miles off-shore. Two men generally operated them. There was no record of any of the dories ever having been lost at sea, and in fact, they had served as rescue boats on occasions when ordinary lifeboats hadn't been able to reach a wreck. They were the largest standard dory made—twenty-seven feet long, seven foot six wide.

While I was wondering about the St. Pierre dory, in particular how to order one, remove it from St. Pierre, and convert it into a yacht, someone else was doing some complementary thinking. In the next issue of the *Fisherman* appeared a small display advertisement announcing that Staples Boats, Inc., of Ocean Gate, New Jersey, were prepared to build French Dories for $550. What was more, they would build them of mahogany planking on oak frames, which sounded a good deal better than the rough spruce or pine of which the native model would be made. The same issue of the paper published the line drawings of Mr. Gardner's version of the St. Pierre boat, slightly modified to have more beam and curved, instead of straight, side-sections. I wrote at once to Staples Boats, Inc., saying "Tell me more."

I suppose boat-builders know which letters come from serious inquirers. At any rate the letter I received from Mr. Staples indicated that he considered me to be serious. It was a sound guess. Despite some hesitation on Mr. Gardner's part in his next article on whether or not the St. Pierre dory would make a sailing boat, that was my intention. Even if it hadn't been, I think Mr. Staples' letter would have converted me.

It was handwritten on light-blue paper, with the printed letterhead of The Blue Water Yacht Co., above which Mr. Staples had penned "STAPLES BOATS INC."

Dear Sir:

The heavy response to our advert. leans more to Mr Gardner's modified dory—so much so that we will eliminate the true St. Pierre as originally intended.

You no doubt have followed Mr Gardner's article and can see that the original St. Pierre is somewhat easier to build as it has straight side sections whereas the modified type requires curved (sawn) frames and other features which add work and some material therefore the bare modified hull amounts to forty-three dollars more for a total of $593.00 at Ocean Gate.

The frames are full 1¼" molded 3" oak-sides planked ¾" Ph. mahogany, bottom 1⅛" mahogany—stem and knees 3" × 7" oak. Fastened with bronze bolts, bronze screws, bronze ringed barbed nails—monel anchorfast nails, rubber sealer §800 is used for all bedding. (This in itself will nearly hold a boat together.) No steel fastenings are permitted.

As we advertised the $550 price for the St. Pierre we will honor all requests for same but Mr Gardner's modified type, as he explained, is considerably a better— roomier—and actually a stronger hull and we have firm orders for complete cruising models of this boat up to $590.00.

Our offering at the price mentioned is for bare hull carvel planked and with outer clamp (rub rail) installed, seams calked and primed—all non-exposed wood to have three coats of Cuprinol.

We would be very glad to quote you on any work in addition to the hull if you will write giving us all details and we might say that the Acadia 2 cyl 8 hp make and break engine is priced at $611 plus about 10% or less for customs—plus freight not yet known.

In closing we see we forgot about watertight bulkheads fore and aft and about midships—these we install.

Thank you kindly, Sir.

Yours very truly.

Arthur Staples. Pres.

P.S.

We could deliver a bare hull in 5-6 weeks from time of receipt of order as we have given you a number that would precede others to follow your letter and we hold this open for one week from today—our terms are one third cash with order—balance when ready to ship—and you must be satisfied or we will refund.

Hauling to Stonington would be $180.00 but it is very possible that our haulers will be able to carry more than one of our dories in that direction and that would cut the cost drastically.

A model letter. I particularly liked the fact that it wasn't typewritten, which suggested to me that the Staples Boat Co., Inc., was a low-overhead operation, where the savings were passed on to the customer. I didn't mind the Madison Avenue flavor of "heavy response to our advert.," the rubber sealer that would nearly hold a boat together (one hoped it wouldn't have to), and "our haulers." These touches merely seemed to indicate a man who was trying to keep pace with the changing conditions of the market place. I was convinced that I had found my boat-builder. I sent off a deposit of $200, and was given, on the Staples priority list, number 1.

Having proved myself, I contacted Peter Tripp—who had become a neighbor—over the garden fence and asked for his assistance in drawing up plans for a modified St. Pierre. Peter had trained as a draftsman. He rented one end of the old New York, New Haven, and Hartford Railroad freight house—

a red-painted, clapboard structure built on a platform of heavy creosoted timber, and raised on piles on the waterfront between Dodson's yard and Longo's Dock. The place was crumbling. The platform was rotten; clapboards were falling off; windows were broken. However, in return for a reduced rent, Peter had fixed up the freight office, so that the door locked, the roof didn't leak, and within, a cheap tin stove consumed large quantities of firewood and periodically threw off great blasts of heat. From a dusty window there was a view of Longo's, of the ramshackle lobster shed and dock of Pi Henry, a part-time lobsterman, and of the brown, early winter landscape of Wamphussuc Point on the far side of the harbor.

3

Designing and Driving

During the first weeks of December Peter and I went down to the freight house at three o'clock in the afternoons and set to work. Out of the piles of charred and sooty equipment that had been salvaged from his burnt Triton, we liberated instruments and drawing tools—protractor, battens, splines, curves, scribing compasses, and "ducks," which are the lead weights used to hold battens and splines in the sinuous shape the draftsman wants to render. In fact, they look more like toy whales than waterfowl. A search among local stationery shops had produced tracing paper, and since it wasn't large enough, we taped sheets together to make the required size. We made a drawing table out of an old door by covering it with a sheet of quarter-inch plywood. Arthur Staples had mailed to us a three-quarter inch-to-the-foot scale drawing of the hull plan, with frames marked in as he was intending to build them, and I produced a sheaf of sketches of more or less what I thought the boat should be, and a short list of features I didn't want to incorporate.

What the terminology of the time would call the central concept was cheapness. The boat was to involve nothing that would be expensive, now or later—she not only had to be a cheap boat to build but also a cheap boat to maintain. (The two requirements are usually mutually exclusive, for a cheaply built boat often costs a lot of money to keep up.) I wanted a boat I could paint and overhaul each year without much bother, a boat that could be run up on a beach for underwater attention or rolled into a field and that wouldn't require a slipway or a boatyard and yard-bills. Her characteristics for the moment were mostly negative. I knew what sort of a boat she mustn't be. Many people graduating from a sailing dinghy to a small cruiser try to ram in as much as they can. They think their twenty-four–foot sloop should have berths for five, a private, enclosed toilet, spacious galley, ample stowage space, and sparkling performance—leaving room in the cockpit for two pigmy-sized crew to run the ship. Yet most people use their boat as a day-sailer for much of the season, taking perhaps a week's cruise of discomfort (when they try to squeeze in the five adults for whom they have berths). It seemed to me that a boat for what is commonly called a young and growing family should be primarily a day-boat, with a large cockpit in which children could crawl, toddle, and even jump around without danger to themselves or the craft, or harassment to their parents. Such a craft might have rudimentary accommodation for two, and perhaps a tent covering the large cockpit. Cooking could be conducted on a small shelf, with water kept in plastic jerrycans, and the toilet facilities should be a bucket. I belong to the school of marine thought that says the less holes through the bottom of the boat, the better. For that matter, most of the tiny stalls containing the flushing nautical water closets I've pumped have been dens for the collection of foul odors and the inducement of claustrophobia and mal de mer.

Because of the requirements of shoal-draft to allow for hauling and also for sailing in thin water, I wanted no keel, but instead a centerboard of a large, strong kind. I thought about having a high, self-bailing cockpit, with scuppers to drain off any rain or salt water that fell into it, which would also be a seaworthy device. But such a lofty, shallow basin would also mean that the crew would be higher in the boat, with less to prevent them falling overboard, and more chance presented of being hit on the head by the boom as we tacked. One luxury I cared for was six foot of headroom under the boom. Furthermore, I thought I'd be happier with the children in the boat if, instead of an ocean-racer's cockpit, I had a floating playpen amidships—even if the playpen had a centerboard case in the middle of it and needed pumping after a night of rain. The cockpit sole was therefore low down on the flat floor timbers of the boat.

Questions of this nature rose and were tackled one by one and sometimes three by three as Peter sprang his splines and battens into shape, and I sat (he had the one chair, befitting the skilled draftsman) on an upturned packing case, varying my distance from the tin stove, within which galactic explosions took place whenever the fire chose not to die. Our design problems were basic layout, the plan of the cuddy, the location of the centerboard, and the style and size of rig. I might also include under the heading "design problem" the ashes from Peter's pipe, which fell onto the transparent tracing paper, got mixed with shreds of rubber eraser, and made little bumps and smudges to irritate the draftsman as—with a tap—he tried to make a spline assume precisely the curve that met our joint approval—"maybe a hair more"—"no, hold it, that's it"—"okay." With this, Peter would run his pencil along the edge of the spline to which I added a hand making an extra "duck." As he moved the pencil forward Peter also rolled it round and round, insuring a uniform black line.

The design of the cuddy was partly resolved by other factors. The need for a large cockpit pushed it forward. Cheapness suggested that it be of the raised-topsides kind, with deck beams spanning the boat from side to side without interruption—this was the simplest arrangement possible. And since the dory was already high in the bow, it seemed to be largely a matter of fairing the lines so that she didn't look bow-heavy, so that the deck of the cuddy was low enough in regard to top-hamper and windage, and high enough in regard to sitting headroom inside. We could gain some of this headroom by giving the deck a good deal of camber. On the other hand, too much camber would make the foredeck a precarious place on which to stand to deal with anchors and sails. We considered all these elements, practical and aesthetic, and hoped we had achieved just the right curve in the sheer of the raised-deck so that it would harmonize with the sheer at the gunwale. In fact, we forgot one element: plywood would not bend two ways at once. This gave the builder the chance to introduce his own ideas on this score.

Armed with a set of our plans, Peter and I drove down to New Jersey in mid-December. We went in trepidation, unsure of what we would find at the other end: a maildrop that gobbled up two hundred dollar checks, or maybe nothing at all, a mirage, or what the old Dutch sailors used to call a "butter island," which melted away as one got closer to it. Mr. Staples' second letter, confirming an estimate of $40 for a centerboard trunk installed, hinted at an assembly plant prefabricating dozens of dories and went on, "we have a lot of dories going to all states in New England ... some will sail home from here—some down to North Carolina, South Carolina, Florida ..." But I had tried to find Ocean Gate on a road map of New Jersey, without luck. Coastal charts didn't show it either. The word among the Greek chorus of old and young salts at Dodson's was that (chuckle, chuckle) I was off on a number one pipedream.

However, a last minute call to a Jersey operator placed Ocean Gate in the vicinity of Toms River, on Barnegat Bay. Peter and I plotted a course and reckoned it a five-hour trip. A factor we took into account was that my wife and her doctor had plotted and reckoned her to be in her last week of pregnancy. It seemed right that our trip should be made in a single day. Working backward, we wanted to be back in Stonington at 8 P.M., which meant leaving Ocean Gate at 3 P.M. Allowing four hours for talk and inquiry, that suggested an arrival time of 11 A.M., which in turn suggested leaving Stonington at 6 A.M. This meant getting up at 5.

For me, there is little romance in the hour. It is the time at which enthusiastic sportsmen rise to blast away at ducks, but it reminds me of rising into a chill, damp nightmare to scrub out the Army barracks where I did basic training. The dawn comes as a friend if it puts an end to insomnia or a cold night watch, but to me, attuned metabolically and perhaps metaphysically to getting up at eight, with difficulty, there's no great bonus in rosy-fingers—my eyes aren't sufficiently in focus at that hour. Peter fortunately was no early

morning hearty. We sat taciturnly over a five-thirty breakfast of eggs, toast, and several cups of coffee. Peter smoked a
cigar. Then we were off, still in the dark, wedged into my
Renault, buzzing down the Connecticut Turnpike, the West
Side Drive of Manhattan (9:15), the Lincoln Tunnel, and
the Garden State Parkway to Toms River. It was a raw day.
Peter puffed cigars, drank three bottles of Ringnes Norwegian
beer (*Ingen pant, ingen retur*, means No deposit, no return),
and talked of Friendship sloops, Novi lobster boats, and
Bristol Channel Pilot cutters. We tussled with the slip-
streams of diesel-exhaust spewing behemoths, paid fees to the
keepers of sundry toll gates, and at last, off the parkway, came
along a drag strip lined with screeching realtors, warring gas
stations, and dine-and-dance banquet inns to a scattered ham-
let of flimsy winterized summer homes. Ocean Gate.

Arthur Staples had hung out his new sign on a post in his
front garden. The grass was occupied by two bright red plywood runabouts, a Hickman sea-sled, and a rather rough,
used lapstrake sports fisherman. To the right rear stood an
off-white bungalow stretched out in one direction to a garage
and a clutch of store rooms. A large concrete barn to the left
rear looked full of dairy trucks and refrigerating machinery,
although the sound of hammering came from within. We
parked the Renault next to a 1949 Cadillac which rested in
front of the barn. Behind the trucks we could make out a
youth of sixteen or so who was stacking sheets of plywood
against the rear wall. A pile of mahogany planks lay in the
shadow of an ice machine.

We found Mr. Staples in his office, in the wing of the
house. He was a small, wiry, middle-aged man with glasses
and a startled shock of gray hair. We caught him on the telephone, discussing the purchase of a pickup truck, but he
gestured to us to find a seat and he hung up quickly. It may
have been that he was as glad to see me, his customer, as I
was to see him, in the flesh. With oblique, introductory state-

ments we reassured each other of the authenticity of the situation. It seemed that at the workshop of a Pennsylvania friend he was mass-producing eleven standard St. Pierre dories. The following week he intended to start work on his first modified St. Pierre. Inquiries were coming in from all over, and frankly, he thought it was too early to say how many would turn into real orders; but it looked promising all right. He had worked in the aircraft business and for a builder of Jersey sea-skiffs before setting up on his own, and he hoped we wouldn't judge him by the plywood runabouts in the front yard. He was prouder of the Jersey power garvey he had under construction in the garage between office and house. It was half-planked up, with massive fir frames that in some places still held bark. Strong and simple was the way Art Staples built boats. No frills, he declared. He claimed, however, to be in touch with modern methods and materials and spoke with a trace of nostalgia for the line-production of his aircraft worker days. Art said his men were off working on another project. I said that, anyway, some of the best boats in the world had been built by a man and a boy. Peter gave me an inquisitive glance, and for a moment I thought he was going to say, What boats? But he didn't.

We moved to the barn, part of which had been leased to a dairyman in what I gathered to have been a poor year for runabouts and sea-sleds. Peter examined the stack of Philippine mahogany boards and pronounced them dandy. I glanced at the plywood, which was marine grade. Art said that he was having trouble getting hold of good well-seasoned oak.

Peter and I drove down the road to a tavern where we had meat ball sandwiches and a glass of beer. We returned to the Staples establishment by way of a road that ran along the Toms River. Then in Art's unheated drawing office, behind his front office, we looked at the design of the St. Pierre, which he had lofted full size on sheets of plywood. He had done this meticulously and had found (as builders tend to find when they "blow-up" the small-scale drawings of a designer) several mistakes in the table of offsets published in the *Maine Coast Fisherman*. This discovery stressed the point that naval architects make, and some amateur builders ignore, that a design must be lofted full-scale before building. An inexactitude of quarter of an inch in a small-scale drawing can be multiplied many times in the actual construction, causing untold bother that spreads to other items and elements. The time spent on hands and knees with chalk and pencil is time saved from trying to make planks and frames fit together the way they weren't quite meant to. We also went over the drawings Peter and I had brought along. We debated outboard wells and the proper height of the centerboard case. Art reminded us of such pertinent details as the size of a sheet of plywood, which is generally four feet by eight feet— the expense of a certain section grew astronomically if we gave it a width, say of four feet one inch. He also flattered us by asking our advice on rig, sail area, and ballast; he wanted to be able to pass on the information to other customers who might conceivably want a sailing dory. We said we would send our final drawings soon. Art said he would quote the lowest possible price on whatever we wanted over and beyond the bare hull. I said—suddenly struck by the idea— that I wanted a yacht for a thousand dollars. Once I'd said it, it became the figure beneath which we tried very hard to keep.

We left Ocean Gate at three, and were in Stonington at eight-fifteen. Some friends of mine were giving a party on East 96th Street in Manhattan, but we stayed on the Jersey Turnpike to the bitter end and came over the George Washington Bridge and through the Bronx to Connecticut. Geography and the highway system helped me eschew the festivities. This was just as well, because my wife complained of slight stomach ache at supper; she said she wasn't hungry. I said that if she were in labor she was out of luck, because I had done eleven hours driving that day and didn't feel like any more. The alarm seemed to be false. However at eleven, as we were going to bed, she decided it was the real thing. I called the doctor, who took some convincing that I—or rather she—was serious. Then we drove to Westerly, narrowly missed being killed by an idiot who turned into his driveway across our lane, and had a second daughter before one in the morning. I put this down here, although it has little to do with a thousand dollar yacht, to let the reader know that it is quite possible for boats to be in the forefront of one's mind all day and then, for several hours at the end of the same day, not to think of boats at all.

4

Building

Sailors are fond of adages. Long foretold, long last; short notice, soon past. Presumably knowledge had to be expressed succinctly and with the right degree of exaggeration on ships of old, for there was often no time for speeches or even the give-and-take of ordinary conversation. One time-honored saying that was passed on to me is that only fools build boats —wise men buy. Although it may have been true in many instances, I didn't think it true in mine. The buyable second-hand boats I saw that cost around eight hundred and fifty dollars (which was the price Art Staples quoted me a week after Christmas) were nothing like as sound or suitable as the dory I got for that sum. Admittedly the dory was only two-thirds finished, and the builder's quotation, including three coats of copper-bottom paint and all Everdur fastenings, got somewhat revised before the day of delivery. (The eventual cost of the dory is broken down in Appendix A.) But it would be difficult to say where else on the northeastern seaboard of the United States one could have obtained a reasonably well-constructed twenty-eight-foot hull, with cuddy and centerboard case, for $850. A Stonington boat-builder told me he would have charged that amount simply for the materials. Furthermore, I don't think Art Staples made much profit on the production.

I was glad to be building. Art and I were soon corresponding on a first-name basis. In January he congratulated me on the new child, said he would like to do as little painting as possible since finishing work was "expensive," declared that the dory would be ready on March 1, and asked for an additional installment of three hundred and fifty dollars. The first modified St. Pierre hull was planked up; I could look at it and have it if I wanted. I drove down to Ocean Gate again. I was impressed by the size of the boat—it was a large step from the sixteen-foot Comet which had been my last command. However, I decided that instead of claiming this hull, number one, I would wait for number two. Trial and error had clearly been among the construction criteria in the first boat, and I assumed the lessons would have been learned for the next. In any event, Art didn't mind. He had been appointed a United States dealer for Acadia marine engines, the Nova Scotia machinery with "make-and-break" ignition that powered the native St. Pierre dories and many similar coastal boats. If you want to put a vessel into reverse with this primitive but efficient engine, you stop the flywheel at top dead-center; if the act is well timed, the engine reverses itself, if not, you go straight through the dock. Art had also received orders for more dories. Two were wanted in California, and two in Maine, one of them to be fitted with a tug pilothouse, which seemed a bit like crossing an elephant with a camel. I made the second payment and checked out with Art the additional drawings Peter and I had done for the centerboard case. We wanted it to be as strong and leak-proof as possible.

In Stonington Peter and I were now engaged, in our design sessions, on the problem of the rig. We agreed that the dory needed a rig with a low center of effort, because with a shallow-draft hull it would help, in regard to stability, to have not too tall a mast. This furnished an argument against the Bermuda rig, which is common to most modern yachts. The tall triangular sails of this rig are most efficient for taking a modern boat close to windward. Since, however, the dory would not have a hull particularly suitable for the task, since the bermuda rig's high mast would make the dory more tender than we felt safe, and since it wouldn't look right on the hull, we turned it down. Peter favored the sprit rig. His own fifteen-foot dory was so rigged, the sprit being, as mentioned before, a closet pole, and although in his case the muslin sail didn't set well, it was clearly the sailmaker's fault and not the sprit's. Thames barges, one or two of which still carry cargoes under sail along the English coasts, are "spritties," and so are many Dutch sailing craft. On the Eastern seaboard in the nineteenth century numerous small workboats were sprit-rigged—Hampton lobster boats, Cape Ann sailing dories, Albemarle Sound net boats, and New Haven sharpies, among others. The sprit is a long spar that stands out from the mast at a small angle and holds tautly aloft the peak of the sail—a spritsail being more or less rectangular in shape. It had the advantage over the gaff rig—the other rig common to shoal-draft workboats—in that it hung off less when going to windward, making less twist between head and foot and allowing the sail to take a more efficient aerodynamic shape. It had a short mast and no boom. It also had the disadvantage of needing a spar that crossed the sail diagonally. On one tack the spritsail would therefore stand away from the sprit in a bellying curve, while on the other tack the sail would be pressed by the wind against the sprit, forming a long ridge with valleys on either side. In a two-masted rig, such as a ketch, this disadvantage is somewhat countered by having the sprit on, say, the port side of the mainsail and the starboard side of the mizzen. Peter thought my dory should be rigged as a spritsail ketch.

There was, however, one other thing to be said against it. The sprit in larger boats is a clumsy spar to handle—even the sprit in Peter's dory put him through some perilous acrobatics. It stands near the foot of the mast in a rope truss, called a "snotter." To lift the peak and flatten the sail, you slide the snotter up the mast; on a larger boat you would haul on a tackle to do the same. And since with a long, unhandy sprit it would be an immense and dangerous chore to lift the sprit in and out of the snotter when going for a day's sail, as Peter did, the sprit remains fixed in the snotter on sizable boats. Instead of lowering the sail when coming to the mooring, furling it, and making it fast along the boom, the spritsail is brailed-up. Brailing-lines haul both sprit and sail toward the mast and hold them there. To reef, one hauls in the lower brailing-lines first, so that the sail is furled like the lower part of a curtain being drawn to the side of the window

while the head of it remains stretched out across the top.
Apart from needing a lot of line, this method of reefing also
ignored the law of mechanics that suggested it would be more
sensible in rising winds to reduce sail from the top of the
mast downward, rather than from the bottom up.

So although Peter made some very pretty sketches of spritsails, with handy-looking brailing tackle, I inclined against
them. What convinced me was that if we wanted spritsails we
would have to get them made. For the time being I wouldn't
be able to afford new sails—that fact threw the spritsails out.
The sails we would be able to acquire, second-hand or as
gifts, were more likely to be old jibs and staysails, it seemed,
and with charity in this case as the stepmother of invention,
Peter asked, rhetorically, What about a rig that used just
jibs? For some time he had suspected that the ideal short-
handed modern sailing craft was the five-masted A-frame
genoa schooner. What the blazes was that? Peter illustrated
his notion. Five-masted schooners used to be common enough.
He'd seen them as a boy, making their way down the Sound.
They had solid masts and an orthodox gaff rig. Well, instead
of pole masts, imagine masts that looked—from a position in
the bows facing aft—like a set of letter "A's." They would
have two solid legs where a normal mast's rigging would be,
and a cross spreader holding them apart. The only rigging
would be one forestay to the top of the first A, a series of
intermediate stays from the peak of one A to the next, and
then a backstay down to the counter of the craft. A genoa
jib would be carried on each mast, tacked down between the
legs of the mast ahead. It would be furled on roller-furling
gear. The mast would provide most of its own support and
allow the sail a clear, uninterrupted luff. To windward and
reaching the sails would be highly efficient, Peter thought,
and downwind, with the breeze coming from directly astern,
he believed the sails could be eased out alternately to port

and starboard, and that the wind would be deflected from one sail to the next as with the blades of a turbine.

A pair of free jibs that were donated to us seemed to indicate the proper providential backing for Peter's plan. I was certainly much taken by it. Under discussion in the freight house we modified the A-frame rig for the dory to the extent of an A-frame foremast (carrying a genoa), and a pole mainmast, carrying a genoa forward and a small bermuda mizzen aft. In this way we had the sail area split between three sails. In heavy weather, with no expensive roller-furling gear, I wouldn't have to make a choice simply between taking down sail A or sail B, which would unbalance the boat, but could take down B, leaving up A and C, or could remove A and C, leaving up B. Wind whistling under the freight-house office door prompted the imagination in the tussle to get down sail. And somehow, getting further seaward, one wondered if the

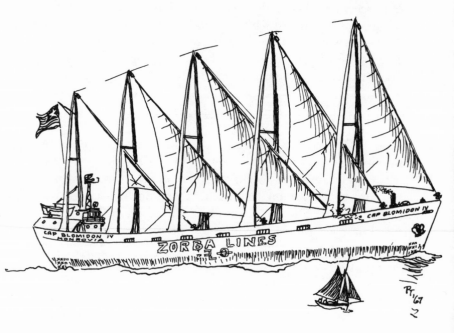

most seamanlike sail of all wouldn't be the Chinese lug, as used by Colonel Hasler on his Folkboat *Jester* in the 1962 and 1964 transatlantic singlehanded races. Fully battened, uncompromisingly square, it furled up like a Venetian blind. It had a great number of strings to pull, however; it would have to be ordered from a sailmaker; and (snow was falling outside) how far was I going to sea anyway?

The building continued. Through February and March Art Staples and I corresponded, and some of his postcards convey the situation nicely.

Feb. 28. Tony, the boat is planked—don't show on your drawing whether Frame 5 goes full across or whether it is only half across—other side full open—think you might have said full with door cut in—how big door?
Sketch please frame 5 showing door etc.
Art.
Way you show it if bulkhead is full to gunnels you crawl over it to enter under hatch and into cabin.

Feb 29. Dear Tony,
Received your card—the painting in the mode you want would be very expensive—suggest you take the semi-gloss white and do the colors as per Van Gogh later—we can do any two-tone at reasonable cost.
Will let you know when hull is complete—probably next week end.
Art.
How will you foot the mast—do you want hole in cabin top and footing block in bottom?

March 2. Dear Tony, thanks for the photos—good. Camber of cabin beam at roof to support jury mast needs going into with you.
Curve of cabin roof line, side view—could this be straight?—Tough to get plywood to do what you show—

but it can be done—though it looks like curve in cabin
roof line would put a belly in the roof panels somewhere
—compound curves.
Standard short forwd deck had same situation on other
dory—tough—we made it but didn't like it.
Cabin should be done one week.
Art

Art's troubles with the design team sprang from our
neglect of the factor of compound curvature, which we had
designed into the foredeck, and which plywood—not fond of
bending in more than one direction at once—doesn't readily
take to. You can see this if you take a flat piece of paper,
representing a sheet of plywood, bend it into a nice curve,
and then try to bend it again at right angles to the first curve.
It buckles. Peter and I had drawn the deck with a good camber, like the convex crown of a road seen from ahead or
astern. We had also (looking from the side) drawn the line
where the deck met the edge of the raised topsides in a
gentle concave curve, and mirrored it with a similar curve
in the beam running fore and aft under the crown. Art es-
tablished our ignorance in a polite fashion and went ahead to
achieve an on-the-spot solution that was satisfactory, balancing camber, crown, and sheer. The one bump that came
out of his working compromise luckily happened to crop up
on the crown of the foredeck, in the precise spot where a hole
had to be cut for the samson post.

Art's question about the mast step concerned the temporary mast we had decided we would need for the trip home
from Ocean Gate. He wasn't particularly enthusiastic about
the A-frame concept and was glad not to be involved in setting it up. We intended to rig a temporary mast for hoisting
a steadying sail on the homeward journey under outboard
motor power; and this spar could be stepped simply in a
wooden chock over a cabin beam. We sent sketches explain-
ing the cabin entrance. The paint job was more complicated.

It was the sort of thing (as Art had said) that he preferred to leave to customers. However, he had included the paint work in his quotation to me, and since then I had got the fancy notion of making the dory look "as per Van Gogh." At college I had hung over the mantlepiece in my study-bed-room a print of Van Gogh's painting, *Barques aux Saintes-Maries* (this wasn't very original of me; most undergraduates had a print by Van Gogh, Klee, or Miro). The painting now came back to me, because it was of French—in fact Proven-cal—dories, hauled up on a beach; they were very nearly the same boat as mine, and it seemed right that my boat should be painted the same colors, flat dark blue and chalky light blue—what Art called "two-tone." I told my friend Yaacov about this and he thought it a great idea. Coming down to Ocean Gate with me to look at the half-completed hull, Yaa-cov told Art that he ought to send out reproductions of the Van Gogh painting to all potential dory customers. Eventu-ally I sent Art—who was a bit confused by all this—a list of proprietary paints that came close to matching those used by the Dutch master, and Art painted the hull with Woolsey Sea Blue, which was a good color, and the raised topsides with a mixture of sea blue and cloud white, which was less of a success. I later covered it with chalky yellow house paint.

Standing in the hull on that visit to the Staples yard, with the sawn oak ribs rising on both sides and supporting the bare mahogany planking which was a light reddish-brown, the color of freshly turned soil, daylight shone through the seams between the planks where calking had yet to be rammed in, and I began to get a sense of the boat, and of how big and how strong she would be. I also began to get the perhaps overdue feeling of how much would need to be done to finish her, or even put her in seashape, after Art had handed her over to me.

April 8. Tony, you would be far ahead to trailer home—could put her where you could do the work much better

—tough to work while overboard—also the remaining painting much easier to get at.

Did not paint cabin top—better you have it bare to fiberglass which I would certainly do.

Too much work before sailing—rudder—c/board—lights —interior paint—sole and deck etc.

Will give you odds and ends of wood for mouldings, trim, shelves, etc.

Art.

This card came in response to a card from me to Ocean Gate, saying that we were rethinking our plan to bring the dory home on her own bottom. Indeed, we had quickly rethought it. It seems curious now that I ever believed such a voyage possible. Peter and I had talked blithely about spending a week in Ocean Gate, knocking together a rudder and tiller, bolting on a spar to carry an old piece of canvas as a steadying sail, painting whatever had to be painted, fastening on a few cleats here and there, launching her in the Toms River as soon as the ice broke, waiting a day for the planks to swell, and then setting off for eastern Connecticut under Seagull power. Outside route via Montauk? Perhaps not. We would go up past Sandy Hook and through the Narrows into New York harbor. We planned a stop at the 23rd Street Marina in Manhattan for a dockside celebration party and the opportunity to take our city friends for a trip on the East River. Then next morning we would head through Hell Gate for home.

I can no longer pin down the turning-point. Perhaps it was simply an acknowledgment of the approach of delivery day in late April. One afternoon Peter and I were talking about delivering the boat by water and the following afternoon we were talking ourselves out of it. Suddenly there seemed to be plenty of reasons not to. The discomfort and the inconvenience—the cold, the need to rely on sleeping bags and buckets and tarpaulins for shelter, a Primus for cooking—were not (we told ourselves) among the reasons. It was simply that we now realized there was too much to do in a week, possibly in a month. Even if we tried to get it done in a short time while living in some ghastly motel in Ocean Gate, what we did would probably be done hurriedly and not well. We wouldn't make a workmanlike job of—and suddenly the list was longer—skeg, floorboards, samson post, cleats, lockers, chain-plates, varnish, rudder hangings, and so forth. For the well-being of the boat, it would be better to do things properly; it wouldn't be a good idea to soak areas of bare wood, such as the foredeck, that were soon to be fiber-glassed. And what if it came on to blow a gale somewhere off Manasquan Inlet? What kind of ballast would we have on board? Would the Seagull (all of four husky horse power) drive her into a bad sea?

I wrote an apologetic note to New York calling off the harbor trips and shipboard party. In reply I received one letter that suggested I was probably too chicken to launch my strange craft in a boating pond, and a second that proposed I trailer it through New York and donate it to the zoo as a Noah's Ark.

5

Delivery Voyage

The preparations were complicated. A trailer was needed, and after much inquiry we found one in nearby Mystic, belonging to a man with a twenty-four-foot centerboard cruising sloop. He paid for the upkeep of the trailer by renting it

out when he wasn't using it. My friend Charles Storrow had recently brought his ancient Star boat, *Sam*, from Martha's Vineyard to Stonington on this trailer, and recommended it —the only aspect of it he hadn't liked was the hydraulic brake, which worked from a handle and pump attached to a piece of plywood jammed under the driver's seat and connected by a length of flexible tubing that ran out through a window of the car to the master cylinder on the trailer. Charlie hadn't taken to this rig, but the owner said the brake worked fine if "you knew how to operate it." I took instruction from him in the operation of it and arranged to rent his trailer for several days, for ten dollars.

Finding a towing vehicle proved more difficult. My Renault and Peter's Volkswagen were both too small; in tandem they might have managed it. Peter's wife Mary had the embarrassed look of someone wondering how to say "no" when we started alluding to her Chevrolet two-door sedan. Any car we borrowed would need a towing hitch properly fastened to the chassis, and not just strapped to the rear bumper. It seemed we would have to rent a car thus equipped. I advertised in the local paper in an attempt to undercut Avis and Hertz, but since this did not produce any response I was glad to hear from another friend, Bill Robinson, in Rumson, New Jersey. He was going off to the Bahamas for a couple of weeks to get the end of a metropolitan winter out of his system, and he suggested that I use his station wagon, which he usually drove daily back and forth to Red Bank station. It was already set up with a hitch for towing his small cruising sloop. And it didn't really matter what damage we did to the car, because it used as much oil as it did gas and was on the point of falling apart.

The next problem was how to get Bill's station wagon. We attempted to coordinate our activities so that we were both in New York with cars at the same time, so that we could swap them. Since this didn't work I drove down to Rumson

one fine day—it was nearly three-quarters of the way to Ocean
Gate—and exchanged cars with Bill's daughter, Martha. She
pointed out to me a mass of various-sized trailer hitches under the station wagon's back seat, jumbled up with snow
chains, a spare windshield wiper, and one of those tire punc-
ture repair kits designed for women who can't change tires
on cars without a spare; it had been used. I asked Martha
for the necessary information about oil and water and any
other idiosyncracies of the old Ford, but she simply bade
me Godspeed with the words, "Oh, don't worry—Daddy
doesn't expect to see it again anyway." I managed to make
it back to Stonington to collect Peter and the trailer, so that
we could then return to New Jersey for the boat.

Peter and I assembled the wagon and trailer and drove
them to Palmer's Garage to have the auxiliary brake properly
installed and the trailer braking light connected to the station
wagon's electrical system. The rig came under Charlie
Palmer's venerable eye. After several minutes' cogitation he
said, "I suppose you're not going far with those rear tires
the way they are?"

"Ocean Gate, New Jersey, Charlie," said Peter, who has
had immense respect for Mr. Palmer, ever since he delivered
Peter's Whitehall rowing boat from Maine by pickup truck.
"About two hundred miles each way."

"Hmmm," said Charlie. "Be lucky if you get to New
Haven."

At this point his son Al, who was making the connection,
glanced at me to see if he should proceed with the job. I
avoided his gaze. Next morning in the early dark we were off.

Driving a car with a heavy four-wheel trailer in tow is a
little like carrying a child on your shoulders. It doesn't
seem to require much more effort than is needed for moving
yourself alone, but it makes it easier to lose balance, and it
requires greater concentration when going through doorways

or under branches. On the country roads I experimented with the auxiliary brake, and limbered up my left arm on the brake handle that came up between the edge of the seat and the car door. After one pumping stroke it functioned efficiently—on the second stroke you could feel the flaps going down on the trailer behind, dragging the car to a halt. Peter was happy the brakes worked, but he didn't disguise his overall anxiety. Once we were on the turnpike we cruised at fifty-five. Peter kept looking out through the back window, left ajar to allow for the passage of the brake tubing, in order (he said) to see the trailer was still there, but in fact to catch the first telltale puff of brown smoke and shreds of black rubber flying as a back tire went through to the canvas and exploded. After a while the strain began to show. He had a cigar and a beer, and as we went over the Connecticut River at a hundred feet on the Baldwin Bridge, he said, "How long do you think they're going to last?"

Callously I said, "What?"

"Good God, man!" said Peter. "Do you mean you slept last night? All night long I had Charlie Palmer's words running through my head. 'Lucky if you get to New Haven.' I mean the *tires!*"

"Oh, them. Well, he may be right. But I didn't see any canvas showing through."

Peter's mouth set in a firm line. He stared a long way ahead, as if into the future. To cheer him up I introduced the matter of New Haven oyster skiffs, and how wide a boat should be to allow for safe tonging, and was it true that length as well as breadth was a factor in stability. We got safely past New Haven. We took the New York Thruway across the Tappan Zee Bridge on the Hudson and went southward through New Jersey along the Garden State Parkway. Every now and then Peter said, "Well, they haven't gone yet, have they?" and I gave him a reassuring nod in reply. We reached Ocean Gate at noon.

The dory sat on the front lawn. In the last few minutes of the drive I had the usual case of customer nerves: Would there be all sorts of bumps and hollows in her planking? Would there be places where you could see the daylight through? As we pulled up by the Staples' sign, Peter exhaled a deep sigh of relief, and I glimpsed the dory perched like a big blue slice of melon among the plywood runabouts. I

knew at once that Art had done a good job on her. The foredeck camber wasn't too steep, nor was the sheer of the raised
deck excessively straight. The mahogany coaming around the
cockpit was long and high, and the mahogany hatch-coam-
ings, unvarnished, were a fine red-brown. As I made a closer
inspection I saw that the centerboard case, built of mahogany
plywood, looked rugged and well bedded-down. The cabin
had a surprising amount of room in it. There was a great
amount of space in the stern quarters abaft the outboard
motor well. She was painted up to deck level with Woolsey
sea blue, the color I approved. Art threw into her some long
strips of oak for rub-rails and scraps of mahogany for trim.
I handed him the final check.

It took us an hour of backing, filling, jacking, and wedging
to get the dory onto the trailer. To my eye she looked loaded
a little far aft, but that kept some of the weight off the rear
wheels of the car, and also gave me the feeling that if
the boat came adrift on the sudden application of the brakes,
she would be catapulted over the roof of the car rather than
directly through it. Peter and I lashed her down with half
a dozen manila warps, and, at points of contact with the hull,
wrapped the warps with old dust sheets and fragments of
corduroy to protect the paint work from the friction of the
ropes. Then we shook hands with Art and his young assistant. The builder was probably glad to get her out, making
room for new construction and removing two designer-
yachtsmen from his hair, but he said, by way of farewell,
"Win some races in her and next year I'll build you a new
one free." Since I believed it quite possible that I should
win a race in her, I tried to indicate by not too smug a smile
that I appreciated the remark but realized it contained a
promise to which no one would hold the maker.

Outward bound, we swung along the Toms River, testing
the rig under load. The sun was out, the river was no longer
iced over, and I was glad the dory was right behind me in-

stead of in the Staples' yard, being rushed into fit state for
a river launching. I stopped briefly and checked the ball-
hitch coupling and the safety preventer of heavy galvanized
wire I had rigged in lieu of chain between the car chassis and
the trailer frame. There was still no canvas showing through
the tires. In fact, I thought on this close inspection that I
could actually see some tread. This encouraged me—not, of
course, to think that the tires were improving—but to realize
that it hadn't been faith alone that had brought us there.
However, I judged it sensible not to mention the matter to
Peter. Driving again, I got used to the new pressures needed
on brake and accelerator and to the presence in the rear-view
mirror of a lunging-forward blue prow. With only a few as-
saults on the patience of local drivers, we wended our way
along the strip of gas stations and diners, around several
sharp bends in the town of Toms River, and across the bridge
to the highway up the Jersey Shore.

We were planning to anchor for the night at the Robinson's in Rumson. Thus we took the route along the shore,
rather than up the inland parkways. Indeed, I was appre-
hensive about the turnpike authorities, and what they would
think of the setup. Eight feet is the maximum width permitted on highways, unless a special permit has been obtained. That was supposed to be the dory's beam, and I had
told Art to leave off the rub-rails so that we would be a few
inches safely inside it. Even so, I didn't dare spring a tape
measure from gunwale to gunwale in case Art had made a
generous error in this dimension. (As it turned out, he had;
later that summer I measured the boat and found her ten
inches longer than twenty-seven feet, and eight foot two *inside* the rub-rails, total beam eight foot four.) I knew
vaguely that there was also a maximum length allowed for a
car and boat-bearing trailer, and I hoped we fitted within it.
My doubts, at any rate, had a suitable background in that
strip of towns along the shore, which always strikes me as

having the slightly lawless aspect of the 1920's, with rumboats hovering just outside the three-mile line and big-time gamblers in the beach hotels. We drove north through Brielle, Point Pleasant, Bay Head, Deal, Asbury Park, and Long Branch, past rows of still boarded-up summer houses and rows of sport fishermen laid up in boatyards. A strong breeze was blowing up Barnegat Bay, and processions of white caps traveled north with us. We didn't travel much faster than the waves, it seemed, but we were in no hurry, and anyone who got stuck behind us for a while, waiting for the opportunity to overtake, appeared to find enough to interest them in the boat for the time they were there. Small children pressed their noses against the windows of passing cars. As we stopped for a light in Sea Bright, a man driving the other way slowed down and shouted, "Say, is that a West Coast surfboat?"

I shouted back, "No, it's a St. Pierre dory."

"Well, it looks just fine."

There had been a fire in Sea Bright the night before, and hoses were still being played on the burned-out shell of a grocery store. Peter and I moored across the street and visited the surviving victualer, who was naturally doing twice his usual business. We bought wine, chops, frozen vegetables, and fresh Italian bread. Then we headed across the Shrewsbury River to Rumson and parked outside the Robinson homestead on Waterman Avenue, which is neatly named. At spring tides, with a spring gale, and an onshore wind, the river rises high, and the Robinsons—who collect small boats the way other people collect cars or cats—float in and out of their house. On this particular evening the river hadn't quite come over the bulkhead. Peter and I waded across the soggy garden and were let into the house by Martha, who came over from a friend's house where she was staying in her parents' absence. She showed us around the kitchen and leaving, remembered to say, "Oh, Daddy keeps the rum in that cupboard by the bookcase." Peter had once, for a brief period, been a high school teacher, but this last considerate remark of Martha's made him take back a number of things he'd formerly said about the American teen-ager.

We were off at eight the next morning in a light rain, taking the road through Atlantic Highlands to the Garden State Parkway. Peter started worrying again about the rear tires. Mud sprayed up from other cars, and when the windshield wipers failed just south of Perth Amboy, he was sure it was the first indication of the shape of things to come. We had new wiper blades installed at the first garage we came to. I then asked the attendant to check the oil, and to allow him to do so pulled the hood release lever under the dash. There was a snapping sound. The lever came back several inches. The hood remained locked. The cable had snapped. The attendant said, "It's a two-hour job springing the lid of one of these things." I told him not to bother. I couldn't remember if I had mentioned to Peter the oil gluttony of the vehicle, and hoped I hadn't.

We got on the parkway, and Peter kept a weather eye open for police and Coast Guard, who—he was sure—had been tipped off by now and were converging on us by car and helicopter. Our cruising speed was forty-five. I found that at fifty the trailer began to sway back and forth, causing the front of the station wagon to shimmy. A slight increase of pressure on the gas pedal, taking us to fifty-five, seemed to reduce this conga motion, but I thought it advisable to remain on the slow side of the wobble barrier. At the first tollbooth no portcullis was dropped. The toll attendant mechanically counted axles, multiplied by fifteen, and charged us sixty cents to pass through. We steamed north through Jersey, and in the latitude of New York City could see the tips of the tallest skyscrapers, peering over the bedraggled Palisades on the eastern edge of the Meadows. Parallel with the unseen Hudson, we ran between the green embankments of the parkway.

The thin rain cleared away, and the sky became that intense light blue—almost black if you look at it long enough—of a fair North American spring day. On the upper stretches of the Garden State Parkway there was little traffic. The tollbooth keepers were unharassed and human. One said, as he handed me my change, "What do you call that?"

"A dory."

"European?"

"French, by way of Canada, by way of Ocean Gate, New Jersey."

"But will she float?"

We laughed and drove on, turning east on the New York State Thruway to the Tappan Zee, where in Dutch days ships sailed and now an awkward bridge sprawls across the expanse of water. We motored slowly over it; I felt the presence of the dory's true element many feet below, and hoped this was the only time she would get this high above it. We came to a halt at a long barrier of tollbooths where lights flashed and signs made bright, baffling indications. We nosed into a slot and I handed two dollar bills to a young black official, wearing a severe uniform and pilot-like dark glasses. He gave me a swift appraisal and studied the car, trailer, and boat. "Move her ahead six inches!" he commanded. I did as I was told, noticing a white line, painted across the lane, to which I brought the front wheels. The official picked up a microphone. "Control, control," he said. "Station six calling control."

"Hullo, six. This is Control." The returning voice seemed to come from on high.

"Control, how does this rig measure?"

There was a pause, no doubt crucial, while we were scanned from a lofty lookout with telescopes, radar, and infrared spectrometers. Apparently we had passed out of life and into a television program. I waited for the oubliette to open and the sudden fall—a rush of wind—a huge, almighty splash.

"Hullo, six. Okay from here. Pass him through."

The official handed me sixty-five cents change and gave us our clearance with an abrupt nod.

"Checkpoint Charlie," said Peter.

The significant events of the rest of our run were a stop for lunch, where we parked our outfit among the big tractor-trailer truck combinations in a Savarin parking lot and ate the lunch of hungry, unparticular drivers; a period when we got the rig through the wobble barrier and cruised for an hour at fifty-five, which was as fast as the dory would ever go; and the moment, somewhere just north of New Haven, when it struck me that Peter had stopped worrying about the tires. No sooner had I had this thought than Peter confirmed it, opening up a Ringnes and lighting a cigar, and saying, "Well, I guess if we've got this far on them we're going to make it." He gave a relaxed and happy smile.

I realized at once that it was now going to be touch and go. As long as Peter had been worrying about those bald tires, spinning around in their ever diminishing skein of rubber, I had been absolved of the responsibility to do the same. Peter's worry had been holding them together. But the moment he was convinced that all was hunky-dory, that we were going to make it, I was sure that nothing could save us. All was lost. Desperately I tried to get Peter to think about the tires by talking of blowouts, overturning, the durability of fast-turning canvas in contact with concrete— but to no avail. Peter was adamant in his belief. His new faith in those tires would have been touching to anyone less certain than I that his faith was misplaced. There was no arguing with a convert.

Peter was justified. At 3 P.M. we reached the "viaduct" that leads over the New Haven tracks into Stonington Borough. Charlie Palmer wasn't out in front of the garage, so he missed the sight of us going by. We made the sharp right turn at the foot of the viaduct and drove through Dodson's yard. The harbor was close at hand, and half way to the freight house Peter yelled the old tug-boat command from bridge to engine room, "All stop!" I gave the hydraulic brake lever a final haul, and we disembarked.

6

Naming

We had already begun to search for a name. It seemed vastly important that we find the right name, though I now see we overestimated that importance. Whatever name one chooses, it may soon be invested with properties one didn't mean it to have; it may lack qualities one had hoped for. Yet, one is impressed by names like *Bloodhound* and *Northern Light,* which seem to evoke the long, lean ocean-racing yawls they are attached to. There is a martial ring of discipline and strength to *Resolution* and *Despatch,* and an inescapable romance in *Malay, Bandit,* and *Finisterre.* Carleton Mitchell claimed the latter as particularly suitable because it had a vowel on the end, useful for hailing purposes, but there was no doubt the word came to his mind in the first place because it suggested the Cape jutting out to sea, the Land's End first to be seen by seafarers at the end of a long ocean voyage. It seems a big step from that sort of name—romantic, allusive—to a type equally favored by seamen, which at first sight appears to be chosen with a decided want of imagination, but which in fact bears witness to close and immediate affection: *Elizabeth Alice, Ebenezer Howard, Brown Smith & Jones.* The poetry is practical. I suppose one should therefore tolerate the modern fashion of abbreviation, often to be noticed on the fat transoms of overpowered motorboats—such names, for example, as *Howmar,* (owned by Howard and Marlene Smith) and *Alsubagi* (created from the first syllables of the names of the Smith's four dogs.) I suppose they are preferable to *Nautigal* and *Winsum.*

I have had my own failures. I called my first boat—a ten and a half-foot Cadet sailing dinghy—*Rhapsody*, which didn't begin to be right for such a snub-nosed, V-bottom, little pram (though it did justice to her fifteen-year-old skipper's feelings about building, owning, and sailing her). I insisted that my father call our slow and most unlively family dayboat, *Caprice.* By the time I reached the ancient Comet on Long Island Sound, the pendulum had swung. Our summer cottage came with a black kitten called Cat. Our laconic Comet was known as *Boat.* I have less irksome memories about the names of the Portchester Duck class dinghies, which were twelve-foot clinker scows with a single dipping lug mainsail, all built by gruff Commander Hammond in his boatshop a few doors away from us. They were excellent boats for the harbor and its muddy creeks, though they tended to bury their noses a trifle dangerously when running before a heavy breeze. Their names had no effect on me as a child, but now seem redolent of the creek, the castle, and the long summer days. They were, of course, all ducks: *Merganser, Shoveller, Teal, Goosander.* The last one built by the Commander was *Surf Scoter,* which he raced himself, and it was a disappointment to him when she didn't prove fast. The Commander once told me that I wasn't sufficiently public-spirited. He did so much to encourage children to sail that he couldn't understand why I didn't take other boys with me, but preferred to sail alone. But I think I was restored to his favor by a solo voyage I made in *Shoveller,* down the creek, out through Portsmouth harbor, along Southsea beach, and across the five mile width of Spithead to the Isle of Wight. I hauled the Duck up on Seaview beach, had a few ice creams for lunch, and then sailed back again, cheating the fierce ebb in the harbor entrance by getting into the eddies right next to the stone fortifications. For a single-handed voyager in a Duck the Isle of Wight had been a far country.

Portsmouth harbor now presents itself in memory as one of those miniature profile drawings that used to accompany charts: the stone forts, the lofty rigging of Nelson's flagship *Victory* in her drydock, the birdlike necks of the dockyard cranes, and the occasional battleship enjoying a respite on her way to the shipbreakers. The Napoleonic hulk of the *Foudroyant* was tethered between two mooring buoys, while across the width of the harbor moved the Portsmouth-Gosport ferry, a sort of floating platform bearing a load of standing people, among which reared an even higher standing brass funnel. There were paddle-wheel naval tugs and the *Shanklin,* an elderly paddle-wheel Isle of Wight steamer—the newer *Ryde* and *Sandown* were twin-screw driven. My father was born at Ryde, grew up on a farm over the downs behind Shanklin, and in prewar summers took us to spend our holidays with my grandmother, who lived at Sandown. We went by paddle steamer. Bells rang, pistons thumped. There was a smell of tea from the third-class saloon, a smell of oil from the engine room, and the clang of shoes on chequered steel plating underfoot. Polished brass plaques gave the date of the ship's construction by Mr. Denny on the Clyde. On the deck, the wooden seats had ropes looped along them, indicating their possible use as life rafts if the steamer sank. A few years ago it was still possible to see, at the Tate Gallery in London, similar seats in the large rooms where the spectacular Turners hang, showing fire at sea and great storms; slatted seats that were robustly curvaceous,

combining the properties of heating ducts and places to sit, and looking like roll-top desks turned inside-out. Indeed, at the Tate one could rest on them opposite an appropriate Turner and, hearing the Tate boilers below, imagine oneself on the deck of the old *Shanklin*, thrashing her way across Spithead toward Ryde Pier.

Although it was never too rough on the trips we made, it was sometimes too early, in regard to the tide, and taking a short cut across Spit Sand the steamer would ground momentarily and have to wait for the assistance of the flood. Then the regular passengers would smirk at one another and throw accusing glances at the bridge. The captain—I used to wonder if it mattered to him—had the gold letters SOUTHERN RAILWAY on his cap.

For a child, as perhaps for adults too, the Isle of Wight was the seaside rather than the sea: it was beaches, piers, sand castles, small towns with curving streets, and shops with sweets, postcards, and spades and buckets in them. And now, if forced to choose between the sea and seaside I would say I like the seaside more. I have no ambition to cross oceans in a small boat, either to make long passages to windward against North Atlantic gales or to scoot day after day down-

wind, rolling horribly, before the beneficent trades. For me
the sea is seasickness, and weariness, and the readiness to
admit "This is it—I'm through." The sea is continual wet-
ness and apprehension and often an absolute terror, and the
fact that one is experiencing it not to make a living but for
"pleasure" adds an element of madness to it. To my mind,
there is more to be said for sailing in shallow water, making
use of the eddies along beaches and watching the current
swirl through the sand; or to pole through marsh channels
with eel grass stroking the topsides and the smell of mud
fairly high. I like wharves and jetties and, living in America,
I miss piers—those quaint iron structures, the last push of the
Victorian railway-building age, poking out from the land,
with bars, amusements, cafés, windbreaks for anglers and
sunbathers, and a theater on the seaward end where come-
dians treated holiday audiences to the corniest gags of the
previous fifty years. You could stand on a pier in a storm
and look down through the cracks in the decking to watch the
sea rising and falling like a concertina, and thank goodness
you were not out on it. In America, on the other hand, I like
the relative lack of promenades and beach huts. I like the
possibility one has of walking, say, from Watch Hill along a
curved sand beach, with dunes on one side and sea on the
other, half the width of Rhode Island. As Matthew Arnold
made clear in his poem *Dover Beach,* the shore is as good as
the sea for somber philosophy—perhaps a little better, for
the sea gives one a large foretaste of eternity, and one can
readily turn back to the land for the mortal present.

Is this a long way from the names of boats? I believe a
name, like a title, should be a touchstone indicating some of
the qualities one hopes the named object will possess, and
at the same time perhaps recreating or at least recalling a
moment past. I like the names *Shoveller, Vol-au-Vent,* and
Tristram Shandy, the hero of which novel is nine months
and several hundred pages being born. It seemed to me a

good name for a comic sort of boat on which one would make picaresque voyages, at any rate to France. Since the dory was an impromptu sort of craft, I felt it needed not too dignified a name. Margot said one day, "How about Bellerophon, or rather Billy Ruffian?"

She explained that *H.M.S. Bellerophon* was the British warship on which Napoleon formally surrendered in 1815 after Waterloo. The British tars aboard her called her *Billy Ruffian*. Bellerophon himself I looked up in Robert Graves's *Greek Myths*. He had managed to survive the day-to-day troubles of a Greek boyhood in Corinth—two murders (one his brother) and the misfortune of not knowing whether Poseidon or Glaucus was his father—only to have Anteia, wife of the King of Tiryus, fall in love with him. When Bellerophon honorably refused her, she accused him of having tried to seduce her. Her husband Proteus, however, didn't dare risk the vengeance of the Furies by liquidating Bellerophon on the spot, but sent him on to Anteia's father with a sealed note saying "Pray remove the bearer from this world; he has tried to violate my wife, your daughter." But Anteia's father was also a king and similarly reluctant to kill a household guest. He therefore asked Bellerophon to do a chore: namely, get rid of the chimaera, which was a fire-breathing she-monster with a lion's head, goat's body, and serpent's tail. The king didn't doubt that the chimaera would take care of the young upstart from Corinth. However, Bellerophon tamed Pegasus, the flying horse, and strafed the chimaera with bow and arrow, finally thrusting a lead-tipped spear into her mouth. The monster's fiery breath melted the lead, which (writes Graves) "trickled down her throat, searing her vitals."

Anteia's father was, of course, ungrateful, and sent off Bellerophon to battle the Solymians and Amazons. From the back of his winged steed, our young hero successfully bombed them with boulders. In the next reel, the king attempted to ambush Bellerophon, but Poseidon came to his rescue and flooded the plain; as Bellerophon advanced on the king's palace, the waves advanced with him. Nothing appeared to stop him. As a last resort the women of the country were called for and lifting up their skirts, they rushed forward, offering themselves to him one and all. At this point, Bellerophon—still a modest fellow—lost his nerve and ran.

But the king had now seen the light. He had been given the truth about his daughter's conduct. He made Bellerophon his heir and gave him another daughter for his own, taking a moment to praise his female subjects for their resourcefulness. Bellerophon thereupon lost his simple ways and (in Graves's words) "presumptuously undertook a flight to Olympus, as though he were an immortal; but Zeus sent a gadfly, which stung Pegasus under the tail, making him rear and fling Bellerophon ingloriously to earth. Pegasus completed the flight to Olympus, where Zeus now uses him as a pack-beast for thunderbolts; and Bellerophon, who had fallen into a thorn bush, wandered about the earth, lame, blind, lonely and accursed, always avoiding the paths of men, until death overtook him."

The name *Billy Ruffian* might enable us to avoid some of the misfortunes that came to poor Bellerophon. It lacked hubris and had a jaunty, raggamuffin ring. It would do well.

7

Finishing

Dodson Boatyard's operating policy is to allow customers to work on the decks and interiors of their craft; the major work is to be done by the yard. This policy was in the back of my mind as we drove in with the dory and Peter said, "Where are we going to dump her?" Down by the freight house we would be on the no-man's-land of the disused railroad property, able to do what we liked without inhibition, but, on the other hand, rather a long way from essential supplies. When Johnny Dodson came out and said, as he admired her, "Why don't you put her next to our shed there—she won't be in the way—and you're not going to be long, anyway, are you?" I wheeled the trailer round next to the shed. Peter and I jacked her up on old blackened balks of railroad sleeper and then slid the trailer out from under her. The return of the trailer and Bill's car was another day's work, enlivened only by the oaths of the garage mechanic who "sprung" the station wagon hood to install a new release cable. The oil was low, but not perilously so. The tires held on that fourth journey.

I took a five-day rest from boats in which I got some work done. I walked down to the boatyard in the evenings to look at the dory and bask in the general sentiment that I had certainly got my money's worth. But dory work also had to begin. Already people were beginning to ask, "When are

you going to put her in?" To be on what I thought was the safe side I answered, "Oh, a month or so," and got on with the labor of bending on toe-rails and rub-rails, and fiberglassing the foredeck, which was a job I accomplished despite several conflicting theories offered to me on the easiest and most efficient way of doing it. There was no clean way of doing it. I began by wearing rubber gloves, wielding brush, roller, and a broad plasterer's knife to squeeze the bubbles out of the resin-soaked glass cloth. I soon had one glove stuck fast to the brush, which had to be discarded because it was firmly planted in a quart of resin in which I had poured a little too much hardener—it had "set" in five minutes instead of fifty. Moreover, I had resin in various stages of cure fixed to my elbows, forearms, face, and hair. George S. Kaufman once wrote a short piece called *Honey on the Telephone,* in which the narrator, putting honey on his toast at breakfast, was called to the telephone. Some of the honey was accidentally transferred to this instrument and soon, from that source, was all over the house. My foredeck experience was the sequel to the Kaufman tale. Meanwhile, visiting experts came over and asked me what my methods were, whether I favored Dynel nylon cloth or Owens-Corning glass cloth, had I heard about Vectra the new miracle polypropylene fabric, wasn't Epoxy resin better than Polyester even with the price difference, and surely monel staples fired from a staple gun held the cloth down best so that it didn't slide around and wrinkle and get those huge bubbles under it? I was using ordinary lightweight glass cloth, the cheapest Polyester resin, and copper tacks. After a while the copper tacks began to stick to the head of the hammer and refuse to stay in the deck. I found it hard to judge how much resin to spread in an initial coat before laying the cloth down on it. A second coat of resin followed, thick enough to fill in the dry patches but not so thick the resulting deck would be glossy smooth—I wanted the impression of the cloth to come through, providing a safer working surface for sailor's feet. In places the cloth slid, and bubbles that I thought I'd flattened out reared up again. I started using my bare hands, and curious rashes broke out on the skin. I vowed never to touch the evil stuff again.

One aspect of amateur boatbuilding that is rarely discussed is volunteer help and advice. You often have to put up with the latter ("I found the best place for a cleat was right under the such-and-such") in order to obtain the former, and there are jobs, like fastening rub-rails and chain plates, where a second and a third pair of hands are more necessary than any tool. Some people want to give advice only, and you have to learn how to go on working while they talk; how to acknowledge compliments or skepticism while—for instance—lying flat on the "floors," which are upright one by threes, and feel like a medieval rack, bruising ribs and knees as you bore out the limber holes the builder forgot; and how to say goodbye and thanks for stopping to see the boat without letting even a hint get in your voice of "Thank God he's going."

In fact, the dory couldn't have been finished without the assistance and gifts of boat-minded people. Every other afternoon I would arrive at the yard to find that someone had thrown into the open hull—the way people throw books into the lifeboat collecting station at Rockefeller Center—a pair of mainsheet blocks, an old jib, a length of stainless steel rigging wire, a hank of shabby but still serviceable nylon line. Much of what didn't come in this form, as donations to the cause, I managed to invent or scrounge. In both categories, I had the exemplary assistance of Arthur W. Smith, known to his friends as Smitty, who was a paint merchant, overhead garage-door salesman, and quartermaster-sergeant-major at the Hiscox Lumber Company in nearby Westerly. Smitty went to sea as a young man on the *Altina M. Jagger*, a coasting schooner that traded between Westerly and New York. He was also a crack downwind helmsman of the Herreshoff fifteen footers that race in summer out of the Watch Hill Yacht Club, and come jousting with each other and the tide along the shore of Sandy Point in Little Narragansett Bay. The Parker brothers take the helm to windward, and hand over to Smitty after rounding the mark. Smitty had seven children and a fine New England knowledge of the art of making a little go a long way. I first met him when racing on Johnny Dodson's schooner *White Wing*—it was a race otherwise notable for lack of wind and lack of beer, unthoughtfully forgotten by the crew member in charge of provisions. Smitty liked the idea of the dory; he offered to help. I bought some lumber at Hiscox's and pretty soon became a regular caller there, for Smitty would take a moment to show me how to deal with a tricky carpentering problem, or would shave a piece of lumber to the right size. Some days I would ride around with him in his old Chevvy pickup truck while he made his calls on Watch Hill gentlemen who wanted birdbaths delivered or rustic fences built. On the front seat there was always an interesting pile of papers, including overhead garage-door literature and yacht measurement forms of the Off-Soundings Club, for which Smitty was one of the official measurers. Occasionally we stopped off on the way back to Hiscox to acquire something for the dory—some scrap lead pipe from a junk yard, or a piece of oak that Smitty just happened to know wasn't wanted somewhere. One day I was in need of chain plates, the metal straps that are securely fastened to the hull and have attached to them the ends of the shrouds, thus transferring to the hull the pull of the sails and spars. Smitty had an idea that the Narragansett Electric Company might be of service.

We drove through the yard gates, on the outskirts of Westerly, turned left, and parked, with the motor running, next to a large heap of galvanized bolts, plates, straps, and variously shaped iron fittings. Apparently they had been in use on utility poles until removed because of a spot of poor galvanizing or a touch of rust.

"Now, what do you need?" said Smitty, like a good host.

I found four steel straps that would do for chain plates. I found a large steel fitting that would make a dandy mast tabernacle if the dory was ever rigged with a lowering mast. I collected a dozen galvanized bolts, all in good repair, and I was picking up the nuts for them when I heard a car drive in, slow down, and halt right behind us.

"Looking for something?" said a man's voice.

I didn't dare look around. If the pile of fittings had been sand I would have stuck my head into it.

Smitty spoke up, disarmingly, "Something to steal."

There was a pause. I looked up. Man in business suit, important big car.

"Help yourselves," he said. He drove away.

I asked, "Who was that?"

"President of the company."

On the way back to Hiscox my nervousness caught up with me. I said ungraciously to Smitty, "What the hell are they doing throwing all that good stuff away?"

"It's cheaper to put on new stuff than to repair or clean the old," Smitty said. "America."

"God bless her."

Some evenings Smitty and I made such parts for the dory as the centerboard, tiller, and rudder. The latter had been lofted full scale on our living room floor, using sheets of brown wrapping paper and soft black crayons. Peter, Smitty, and John McVitty, an architect, all took turns at the design, and we compromised on a rudder that would be strong, with plenty of lateral plane, easy to build, and able to be hoisted, thus reducing the dory's draft when beached or grounded. Both the rudder and centerboard were made of two thicknesses of three-quarter–inch exterior fir plywood. This was glued together with waterproof glue and fiberglassed all over.

Clamps and setting temperatures were crucial, and the chilly
May night we put the centerboard together in the unheated
lumberyard workshop, we had to make a quick dash with
the cumbersome object to the Hiscox office-building furnace
room, where we left it in the warmth. It was cumbersome
partly from size, and from the big clamps sticking all around
the edge, and also because it now had fifty pounds of lead
ballast sandwiched inside it to make it drop. We had taken
the scrap pipe and melted it down with a propane torch,
being careful at the bends and kinks because old pipe may
have water trapped within it, which under heat will boil
and explode in a scalding burst when the pipe melts. We
poured the molten lead into a rectangular flat cookie sheet,
roughly twelve by fourteen inches by three-quarter inches.
Then, when the lead refused to be turned out of its mould,
we put the whole thing into the cavity we had routed-out in
the bottom of the centerboard. The lack of precedent for this
we preferred to think of as a unique quality—not many boats
have an aluminum pan as an essential part of their ballast.

Other items had their own histories. We laminated the
tiller with thin strips of fir, offcuts found in the Hiscox scrap
heap; we gave it a sinuous, functional shape, and the result
was beautiful. The main boom was a simple fir two by three
house stud, twelve feet long. The fittings for the centerboard
pivot bolts, providing a watertight but accessible flange in
each side of the case, were ordered from a Providence plumb-
ing supply company and (to meet our now desperate
schedule) picked up by Smitty and me from the company
director's doorstep in Cranston at 11 P.M. one night. A suitable mainmast was harder to find (we had now recanted the
A-frame heresy and were—partly because we hadn't received
the expected flood of suitable old jibs—planning to rig her
as an orthodox gaff ketch). I called all the local boatyards in
hope of finding an old spar, and eventually I began to think
I'd better try for a flagpole or perhaps another lamination,

if we could get hold of some decent spruce for it, which seemed unlikely. Then Charlie Storrow said, "Why don't you ask James Kleinschmidt at Mystic Seaport? They know all about gaff spars." There the search ended. Jim Kleinschmidt turned up on a surplus pile the boom from a Hudson River iceboat, circa 1860. It was spruce, twenty-eight feet long and six inches in diameter, weathered a grainy black and with a row of heavy screw eyes running along it for the foot-lacing of the iceboat's mainsail. It was a massive spar, which had rested on the rafters of a Hudson River carriage house for seventy-five years and had been lying around the seaport for at least a dozen, dispossessed of its craft. Kleinschmidt (who was the seaport's assistant curator and the owner of an antique cat-ketch-rigged Hampton lobster boat) said, "Take the boom and give the Seaport a small contribution." Smitty and I carted this hefty piece of salvage back to Stonington. I unscrewed the screw-eyes, hammered out several black-iron bolts, and swore to Johnny Dodson—who had rashly offered the use of the boatyard machine planer—that there wasn't any metal left in the spar. One afternoon Johnny, Yaacov, and I made a four and a half-inch diameter mast of it. We ran it through the planer, giving it eight sides, and then, having moved it to the bench, we went to work with wooden hand-planes to make it round again. The result was a hundred-year-old butter-colored spruce spar that looked brand new.

Yaacov was a welcome addition to the force, and indeed his abilities as a "liberator" of gear and as an ingenious handyman seemed to flourish in the Stonington atmosphere, where the old New England do-it-yourself spirit hadn't for some time been seen in such vivid form. Yaacov just then was working as an assistant producer on a TV program in New York. However, he had served in several navies. He had been bombed and torpedoed on the Murmansk run. As a boy he had crewed briefly on a melon dhow in the eastern Mediterranean and once had been chased up the mast by the mate, who was so high on hashish he thought Yaacov was a houri. When I first met him in Manhattan he was in love with a sixty-five–foot schooner called *Windermere,* and would spend whole days sitting on a decayed wharf in City Island, gazing at her and plotting how he would buy her. Fortunately, it was one of those romances that didn't come to anything. Yaacov was beaten to the buying line by three young men who intended to sail *Windermere* around the world; they paid several thousand more than Yaacov thought was correct; they spent several thousand more fixing her up; and they discovered a week or so before setting off on their world cruise that her decks were rotten and her rigging needed to be replaced; at which point they packed up.

Yaacov helped not only with the *Billy Ruffian's* mast but with the chain plates, bridge deck, and lockers. He provided navigation lights, plastic jerrycans, lengths of shock cord, and the boat hook. This implement had, as they say of works of art, an interesting provenance. Yaacov had noticed a very pretty girl who lived in a nearby apartment house in Manhattan. He got to know her. He saw a lot of her. Finally the affair came to an end and as Yaacov said his last goodbye to her in the lobby and the doorman-elevator man took her up, Yaacov noticed a fire hook hanging on the wall; it became a souvenir of his romance. Of course, a fire hook is not exactly a boat hook—it has a sharp point, which had to be covered with a rubber cap of the kind slipped over the feet of a steel chair; it was also rather heavy. But when people complain of the heaviness of the *Billy Ruffian's* boat hook we say, "Never mind," and explain that there are reasons why an ordinary boat hook would not do as well. One person who demanded to know the reasons said that he thought Yaacov had seen the fire hook before he saw the girl. I thought this a thoroughly cynical interpretation of Yaacov's generous conduct.

One aspect of this way of acquiring gear, which included such offerings as a slightly used upper-triatic stay from the *White Wing* and a primus from McVitty's old boat locker, was that it increased a hundredfold the pleasure of actually going out and buying something. Yachtsmen who reach for their wallet or checkbook every time they need an item can hardly imagine the thrill I got from paying real money for a hundred and twenty feet of black polypropylene anchor warp fresh off a wooden drum at Wilcox's Fishermen's Supply Store. There was a similar delight in shopping in a New Bedford surplus store, where shackles, lifejackets, oars, and hurricane lamps had to be searched for among piles of radio and used car equipment. For a dollar I got from a Philadelphia mail-order house an indispensable folding canvas bucket, ex-U.S. Army.

May went by quickly, but the skeg went on, the rudder was mounted, and the centerboard hung. The chorus again rose: "When are you going to put her in?" The boats that had been stored nearby were borne off one by one to the water, though sometimes they were hoisted back out again to have a keel-bolt tightened or a seam recaulked. The

weather grew warmer, and the cars driving through the yard created clouds of dust that drifted over my tacky varnish. The FBI agent who had lent me his power saw and shared his iced lemonade with me had launched his power-boat and gone fishing. The seams of the neighboring whaleboat had been sufficiently swollen with water from the boatyard hose for her to be taken to the saltier element. The yard management began to look at the dory as if she were the nautical equivalent of the man who came to dinner. I decided that, ready or not, I had to stop making vague promises. When one frequent visitor asked me for the eighty-fifth time, with a note of barely suppressed irony, "When's the great day?" I said, "The first of June."

8

Launching

Having said this once, I found myself saying it again and again. I went round telling people to come to the christening. Some people had to be told that I meant the christening of the dory and not that of my second daughter, but most got the picture when I mentioned the boatyard and a keg of beer. On the last day of May Smitty and I completed several last minute jobs, such as the samson post, which was a rugged oak four by four, bedded down on the keel, and had a stainless steel rod running horizontally through it six inches above the deck, making a safe fastening place for mooring and anchor lines. Early on the morning itself, Smitty climbed a ladder to bolt on the stem fitting, while Yaacov and I lay underneath the dory slapping a thick coat of poisonous antifouling paint on the bottom planking and the lowered centerboard, and several small boys—the first to turn up for the celebration—gave our work their condescending approval.

In Stonington, if you invite people to come to a party at six, they generally come five minutes before. A crowd had already begun to form as Johnny Dodson fired up the engine of the Travellift, a four-wheel moveable gantry with lifting slings. Half the village seemed to be there, because people had told people and summer people had brought their houseguests, as summer people will. There were thirty children, three nursing mothers, a dozen transient yachtsmen, and several dogs. Four strong men carried the keg of beer with its pump, tubing, and ice bucket. A procession followed the beer, which followed the Travellift, which—with Johnny at the controls—lumbered noisily across the boatyard toward its U-shaped dock. The dory, suspended like a giant blue and yellow boomerang, swung to and fro. Johnny positioned the vessel over the dock and lowered it, until it was a few feet from the water, with the stem-head at shoulder level. The keg of beer was sprung and paper cups passed round. Margot handed the baby to a babysitter and took in her right hand a bottle of Bass Ale, bought for the occasion. (We had been given a bottle of champagne, but we thought we would drink that.) Then she went and stood by the bows of the dory, looking very nervous. Smitty dashed over and whispered to her, "Give it a good hard sock!"

Silence, and Margot said in a loud, high voice, "I name this boat *Billy Ruffian*." She swung the bottle with a solid forehand drive. Green glass and brown foam flew. Johnny, well sprinkled with Bass Ale, lowered away to the crowd's applause, and the dory touched the water for the first time, slipped in a little, then bobbed gently as the water miraculously held her up. The slings sank away. Wood is a buoyant material, as we all know, and the laws of nature have hitherto given no hint of collapsing at midday on the first of June, but the performance of my boat at that moment—actually floating—seemed to me marvelous.

9

Fitting Out

In the manner of commissioning large vessels, we did our fitting-out after launching, but took the opportunity of a trial run, since the dory had to be moved out of the Travellift slip to a neighboring finger pier. It was a voyage made entirely within Stonington harbor. Yaacov, Margot, and the two children accompanied me, Yaacov acting as first engineer, and the Seagull outboard motor acting not only as motive power but as a smudge pot, creating a cloud of exhaust that billowed beneath the helmsman. (I blamed this smoke on too much oil in the mixture, but it turned out to be a defect resulting from using the Seagull in that sort of boxlike well. You can do better for fresh air in the wake of a Fifth Avenue bus.) In any event, the *Billy Ruffian* ran fast, turned nicely and more than nicely once we dropped the centerboard for her to pivot on, and left little or no wake. "Six knots!" exclaimed a passing fisherman in vocal admiration. Well, it may have been just six knots, and achieved without spars, ballast, cockpit seats, and lockers, or for that matter all the gear that collects on a boat and brings her down to cruising lines. But we spun happily around the harbor several times and made a safe return to Dodson's dock.

June went in work: quarter deck, seats, ballast, spars, and sails. One curiously shaped section of the quarter-deck lifted to allow access to a compartment where the Seagull could be stored. Seats in the cockpit covered lockers for water, charcoal, lines, and anchor warps. In the way of ballast, I happened to give a hand to Johnny Dodson the afternoon he decided to excavate several hundred pounds of lead pigs that were stowed under the saloon berths of the *White Wing*, then being prepared for the Marblehead to Halifax race. To add to these, handed over on "long loan," Smitty found twenty iron sash weights, weighing about ten pounds each, which I dipped in red lead paint before stacking them neatly under the cockpit floor. The rig had now been firmed-up, balancing available sails and spars—the sails being two small jibs and

two Bermudan mainsails, which, with their triangular peaks suitably cut off, were converted into a gaff main and a gaff mizzen. The main was a 1949 blue cotton sail from a Lymington Slipway five-ton sloop, a splendid piece of canvas work by Cranfield and Carter of Burnham, Essex, on the East Anglian coast. I took it over to the nearest sailmaker, Sandy Van Zandt, who was in the process of establishing his loft in a masonic ballroom on the third floor above the Noank Universal Food Stores. Sandy was a crack dinghy sailor and a first-rate modern sailmaker, but he suffered with me and my ancient sail, did a job of sewing on the eight-foot head rope that any leather-palmed bosun from the great days of sail would have praised, and put in some useful groundwork toward talking me into buying a Penguin dinghy for frostbite racing the following winter. Margot and I tackled the mizzen ourselves. With some instruction from Yaacov on the proper use of thread, wax, and palm, we made a passable job of conversion of the Murphy and Nye high-aspect-ratio Bermudan sail. We stamped in the grommets, sewed on the bolt rope, and more than once stabbed the needle into opposing fingers. The sails were to be laced to gaff and boom with nylon mason's line and on the luff lashed to mast hoops.

The hoops were a small triumph. Finding a supplier of these (in South Dartmouth, Massachusetts) was difficult to begin with, and his quotation of thirty cents per inch diameter didn't improve matters; for a six-inch hoop this worked out at one dollar and eighty cents, plus postage, and I needed nine hoops for the main and five slightly smaller for the mizzen. However, one morning at Wilcox's Fishermen's Supply Store I spotted, hanging from a rafter, a string of wooden hoops, more lightly built than mast hoops. They were rings used to hold open the net entrance to a lobster pot; they were oak; and they cost ten cents each. They seemed eminently worth it, even if they only lasted several seasons. Before buying them, though, I went to see the manufacturer, a local craftsman called Wolcott Palmer. His workshop stood on a hill, overlooking a stream, a mile backcountry. Indeed, until a year before Mr. Palmer's homemade hoopmaking machine had been run by water power. Now, in his late seventies, he had gone modern with electricity; a small motor turned the vertical lathelike machine as it received the thin strip of green oak and bent it in a five and a half inch diameter circle, stopped, and held it with two ends overlapping while Mr. Palmer, with two deft strokes, clenched the ends with copper nails. Mr. Palmer had worked things out so that he didn't waste motion, and neither did he waste words. I asked him if his machine could be adapted to make a six-inch ring for use as a mast hoop. He allowed as how it could, but thought it might put the price up a fair bit; in fact, he didn't think it would be worth the trouble. He thought I should use the five and a half inchers if I really believed they'd stand the wear and tear. His price was eight cents, but he couldn't sell them to me; that was his deal with Wilcox. So I went back there and stocked up with enough at ten cents each to last a good few seasons.

The fitting-out process was interrupted for the Halifax race on *White Wing*, to which I had promised my services the year before.* Johnny had been working for a month preparing the old schooner. We took her up to Marblehead via the Cape Cod canal, got a good start in our class, and

---

* My reputation in Stonington as an experienced ocean-racing yachtsman was founded on a misreading of a work on that arduous sport by Commander Errol Bruce of the Royal Navy. Commander Bruce was apparently out racing with a man called Bailey, when they were beset by a fierce electrical storm. Bailey offered to take precautionary measures, and was in the act of attaching chains to the shrouds, which he meant to dangle overboard as conductors, when there was a sudden *crack* and Bailey vanished from sight. Well, the rest of the crew thought that was that, God rest his soul. But no—Bailey reappeared from the far side of the doghouse, and remarked, through his singed beard, "The chains worked."

For some reason the owner of a Stonington ocean racer thought that I was that Bailey, and thereafter kept asking me to crew for him in the Bermuda and sundry other races. The fact that I kept refusing him made it seem as if I knew even more about it.

then spent a disappointing first day close-hauled in light breezes, watching the up-to-date fiberglass sloops and sleek forty-foot yawls flouncing away from us. But as night came down, the wind came up abeam, and moved slowly around on the starboard quarter. The Gulf of Maine seas began to rise. The crew was divided into two watches, and I was port watch captain—we were on from eight until midnight. We could see on the port bow the dim lights of our competitors become brighter on the port beam, for our heavier ship was leveling seas that were slowing down the opposition, and we were plunging forward without a pause for breath. We were flying the largest genoa, the mainsail, and—what really took advantage of this schooner weather—the nine hundred square foot balloon staysail, called fondly the gollywobbler, which occupied the entire area between the masts and overlapped a considerable part of the mainsail as well. This was a pulling sail. Indeed, the dacron tail on the windward running backstay shrank under the tension to half its size. Frank Jo Raymond, an artist-photographer who had once been keeper of Latimers Light in Fishers Island Sound and had rowed several times from Stonington to Block Island in a small skiff, helped me back up this strumming vital support of the mainmast with four parts of nylon line. Off on our quarter the white crested seas rushed along, and under the swelling gollywobbler, the bow wave rocked past, occasionally slapping up with a mild explosion into the sail as the *White Wing* dipped and then, as she swung up, cracking free. The main boom, vanged down with tackle fastened to a heavy-duty rubber strap, dipped its clew end into the waves on every other roll.

Then the starboard watch came on deck.

At the time, of course, I couldn't see it, but at this distance it is a little easier to view that scene, as it must have appeared to Peter Tripp, the other watch captain, and his gallant men, as they lurched up on to the deck, rubbing the light accumu-

lation of three and three-quarter hours of uneasy sleep from
their eyes, fastening up foul-weather gear, and suddenly
hearing the howl of the wind and thump of the seas. The
joyful gleam in my eyes, as I sat behind the wheel, could
easily have been mistaken for the look of a crazed fanatic.
The sounds that we had gradually got used to were brand
new and frightening to them. "Good God!" yelled Peter.
"They're trying to drive the boat right under." And telling
one man to sound the bilges and if necessary man the pumps,
and another to take the helm, he led a companion forward
to get down the gollywobbler. The captain was asleep on the
navigation table, taking no sides. I tried to argue with Peter,
but he wouldn't hear me, for the seaman in him told him
that at any moment the old schooner, under the terrific
pressure we had piled on her, would begin to come apart.

This is what happens when you go ocean-racing. I sat
fuming loudly while Peter and his men got the great staysail
down and then actually put a reef in the main. Our speed
dropped from over eight knots to a little less than seven; the
boat surged more gently. A little water was found in the
bilges, and Peter felt justified, and I felt more furious than
ever. Indeed, we had found a situation where our tempera-
ments found a perfectly contradictory expression, and we
were chilly for days afterward. That night I hardly slept,
waiting for my watch to get on deck again at four, so that
we could rehoist the huge sail.

Next day I was sick. A little less wind, more swell, and
perhaps as well the nervousness of approaching Cape Sable
in fog, with Johnny on the radio direction finder getting a
perfect bearing on Cape Cod, several hundred miles distant,
and no bearing at all on the Nova Scotian promontory a few
(though we didn't know how few) miles away. We heard
whistles and fog horns and imagined that we had a fix on
Seal Rock. We were—we later concluded—well inshore, so

much so that no other boats had dared to cut in so close. But we didn't hit any rocks, and the sickness passed.

On *White Wing* I always had the consolation that the skipper got sick before I did, in fact, it was astonishing how anyone who got seasick so easily found pleasure in being at sea. But Johnny did, even though he had stuffed himself with all sorts of remedies at both ends. None of these things worked for me. I still hoped that one day I would find once again that I didn't get sick, having recovered the immunity I'd seemed to have as a child. It was something I'd preserved for a long time, like my disbelief in poison ivy and hay fever. It had vanished in a few minutes one afternoon at the western approaches to the Solent. I was the sole crew, aged fifteen, on a new yacht (designed for singlehanded work in Arctic waters) that the owner was taking down to Falmouth. We got in a lop, with little wind, and the new diesel created fumes that seemed to wreathe me, as I sat trying to concentrate at the wheel. I was beginning to feel odd when there was a sudden glassy crash below. The owner said, "Be a good chap and go and see what that was." It was a bottle of sweet vermouth, fallen out of a cabinet, and lying now in a sticky, shattered mess all over the cabin sole. I made one pass at it with a cloth and then dived for the head.

Smells of many kinds appear to form a powerful trigger, at least with me. Perhaps at sea one's sense of smell becomes more acute, in a similar way to that in which one's sense of balance is supposed to be increasingly disturbed. The smell of cigarette smoke, which I can usually tolerate, becomes insupportable in any kind of sloppy seaway. On the first day of my one and only Bermuda race, someone took the lid off a two-gallon jar of green pickles, which had been swilling around in view of everyone sitting in the cockpit. And that was it as far as I was concerned.

Off Cape Sable we could smell the land, and the tide came

roaring round the corner from the Bay of Fundy and gave
us a welcome boost along the Nova Scotian coast. We found
Sambro lightship with difficulty (two boats overstood it by
an hour and had to turn back), and leaving it hard to port,
trimmed our sheets for a gusty beat to the entrance of Halifax
harbor and the finishing line. Friendly gunfire from a de-
stroyer marked our crossing. On the yacht club porch we
found to our delight that we were third in our class of twenty
boats, seventh out of the entire fifty-boat fleet, and best of
all, that we had won the famous Schooner Trophy, beating
(by some forty minutes when the handicaps were worked
out) the *Niña,* Bermuda champion and the greatest schooner
of them all. Sailors on liberty, we lived it up in the houses of
hospitable Halifax citizens and went to splendid parties on
harborside lawns. In the end, we had to do some loud talking
to get the coveted cup, which someone had polished and put
away.

In Stonington, the problem awaiting me was a leak. In the
age of fiberglass, it is possible that there are readers of this
who may not in the fullest sense know what a leak is. Of
course, plastic boats may get holed. They may be stored for
the winter with water still in their keel tanks and, when ice
forms, split surreptitiously; after launching in the spring, the
question may well be asked, "Why does the drinking water
taste salty?" Fiberglass boats may also run onto submerged
pilings, like the boat that figures in this later on, and be sunk
before anyone has a chance to cram a life-jacket in the hole.
But these aren't really the sort of leaks I have in mind. What
I'm thinking of is altogether less sudden: something you
realize at first only because, when left the night before, there
was just a little water in the bilges, and then next morning
it is sloshing around above the floorboards. In this case, my
wife Margot reported that while I was aboard the *White
Wing,* seeking ocean-racing glory, the *Billy Ruffian* hadn't
"taken-up"; in fact, she had needed to be pumped out every

other day and there was a lot to pump. So I pumped her dry and went investigating along the inside seams, moving from frame to frame, searching the butts that covered the end-joints of planking and examining the centerboard case. I sponged away the water to see if I could find the source from which it came. Finally I thought I'd found it. The water came running along the angle of the starboard chine, where side planking met bottom planking, and appeared to be flooding from a point about midway between frames four and five in a slow but confident stream. And that would have been fine, a real discovery, if I had been sure that this was the leak and not simply the mouth of an underground or within-the-caulking river that had its source perhaps five feet away. (Deck leaks are similar, except that you also *hear* them. Their menace is dramatized by the drip, plop or ping of water falling—falling inevitably where it gets a reaction from inhabitants of the cabin; moreover, it gets you wet.)

My leak was perhaps characteristic. Caused by poor caulking, it was made worse by my attempt to cure it from the inside. I bought a small can of black tarry compound, and then, sponging away the incoming water, plastered this goo along the seam and rammed it in with the edge of a putty knife. When this didn't seem to be having much effect other than to start conveying the compound, like Kaufman's honey, all over the boat, I twisted some strands of caulking cotton in a professional manner and laid them in the tarry crack, where I hammered them in. For a moment I thought I had solved the problem. The leak seemed to disappear. But before I had the cotton back in my pocket and the can of tar properly closed, a real inrush began from forward of frame four. For somehow in blocking the flow at one point I'd forced it to come in even faster at another—a simple matter of the new caulking cotton swelling as it got wet and pushing the already mismatched planking farther apart. I took to the pump. When I saw that I was barely keeping up with the rising waters, I took to the dock, found Johnny, and had the *Billy Ruffian* plucked from the harbor by the Travellift before she foundered.

On land I got underneath the boat and did a better job of bunging up the crack from the outside. The following year I had the chine seams professionally caulked, and after that the amount of water she took in was only enough, as they say, to keep her sweet.

10

Early Voyaging

My delight in the *Billy Ruffian* was sometimes dulled by the sheer desperate hard work of getting it finished. I succumbed to the temptation to go sailing in the boats of friends, like McVitty's Yankee One Design *Broomstick*, which was all set and ready to sail in the late 1940's and has been kept so ever since, and I accepted—not altogether because of sympathy— the umpteenth invitation of the man with the sixty thousand dollar yawl to go out and help him sail her; she had so many sails and chrome gizmos he didn't dare take her out alone. But the day came when the *Billy Ruff*—though by no means finished—was sailable. I hoisted mizzen, main, and jib, in that order. Except for the mizzen, which drooped a little on the foot, they all set well. I backed the jib, dropped the loop of the mooring painter over the side of the bow, and I was loose, if not exactly away. I jumped down from the foredeck, hauled in the mainsheet, and stretching aft, centered the tiller. The *Billy Ruffian* heeled to the light westerly breeze and began to move—at first somewhat sideways, and then, as speed increased her grip on the water, forward, slipping along in the direction I pointed her. How remarkable! The rather haphazard shoreline of Stonington village slipped past as I sailed toward the gap between the breakwaters.

I congratulated myself on all sorts of things that were probably inherent in her character. A dory, a true seaboat, she would have done for anyone what she did for me, but I took as a personal triumph the fact that she left no wake, and rode without bouncing through a chop caused by a passing motorboat. She came about easily. She had no alarming helm; at first, in light air, she had a bit of lee helm, which meant that if one let the tiller go the boat's head tended to pay off from the wind rather than round up into it. Weather helm is safer, providing a sort of deadman's throttle if you fall asleep or overboard, and it allows one to take a boat to windward more efficiently. But this touch of lee helm was cured with a new mizzen mast soon made for her; a higher spar, stepped a little farther aft, and allowing the mizzen to set better. The strong weather helm she acquired on a broad reach in a good wind was easily cured by lifting the centerboard slightly or easing the mizzen. There were other idiosyncracies to get used to. In anything more than a zephyr she sailed to windward at twenty-five degrees angle of heel, which alarmed some fairly experienced sailors. One eminent yacht designer, down in Stonington to see a hundred thousand dollar yacht just completed from his designs, remarked to John Dodson, Sr., that the first thing he would do with a boat like the *Billy Ruffian* was carry out capsizing tests. But in fact she seemed to heel so far and no farther, finding her stability with her gunwale down, and taking in, even on rough days, no more than the odd dollop over her lee coaming. Spray was brushed aside by her high prow, flared sections, and raised topsides. She tacked in an angle of a hundred and ten degrees, which was pathetic if you were used to *Broomstick's* ability to do the same in eighty-five

degrees, but was as good as that of the *Scarlet Rover* and a
pretty gaff-rigged schooner that moored in Stonington harbor.
She wasn't very fast in a ghoster, but she slipped along mer-
rily with a fair wind free.

I had Jeffery Reynolds with me on one early sail. He had
been to Halifax on the *White Wing*, while on leave from
the Marines; he was currently a guard in the brig of the
aircraft carrier *Essex*. Jeffery's skill on the schooner's foredeck
was matched by his cheerfulness in the cockpit on a long
night watch, as he told how the U.S. Navy chased phantom
submarines from Key West to Cape Sable, how some of these
enemy ships turned out to be Gloucester fishing trawlers,
and how Russian fishing vessels would dart across the bows
of the *Essex*, bring her to a stop, and then pan her from stem
to stern with infrared cameras mounted where their trawling
winches ought to have been. It was a reminder that other
kinds of sport were going on out on the Atlantic. Jeffery had
relatives in Stonington, and a girl friend or two, and helped
us peel wallpaper in the front hall in return for dinner and
a bed.

Jeffery and I sailed the *Billy Ruffian* around Stonington
Point and through Wequetequock Approaches on the north
side of Sandy Point, leaving Salt Acres on the port hand. It
was a hot August afternoon, clear close by, but with a

distant haze, and just enough wind from the southeast to fill the sails and keep us moving. We stood close-hauled across Little Narraganset Bay toward the Pawcatuck River. Jeffery exclaimed, "Gosh, she goes okay!" But my enthusiasm was moderated by the sight of a thirteen-foot Blue Jay, sailed by two children just off our weather bow, outpointing us and outfooting us too. However, I soon learned to ignore this kind of performance, and certainly not to try to emulate it. Given a free head the *Billy Ruffian* kept moving and got sooner to wherever it was we wanted to go.

On this excursion we sailed the *Billy Ruffian* past Osbrook Point with its outlying rocks, and several tacks took us into Watch Hill harbor. We admired the summer mansions, the row of elegant shops along the waterfront, and the hotels on the hill. There are people living in Watch Hill who have spent twenty-five thousand dollars on a single party. It is a curious place—a lesser but still thriving Newport, with many midwestern industrialists and Episcopalian clergy in the summer. We dipped round the stern of Avard Fuller's (Fuller Brush Co.) big green ketch, *Diogenes,* swung round in front of the Watch Hill Yacht Club, and, jibing, worked our way through the crowded moorings to the bay again. Jeffery set a course between the dome of the Ocean Hotel and the near end of Stonington east breakwater, designed to take us safely through the shallows or "cut" between Sandy Point and Napatree Point.

Before the 1938 hurricane (which is the way a good number of local tales begin), the island of Sandy Point was connected to Napatree. Fort Road ran out from Watch Hill to the fort at the end of Napatree Point, and was lined with summer houses. It was along this shore from Napatree to Misquamicut that the full force of the storm hit, with thirty-foot waves and more than hundred mile an hour winds. It had been a pleasant breezy September afternoon. One lady afterward described how she sensed the wind coming up, and sent some boys out to check the family boat; pretty soon she saw that it was adrift from its mooring. The breeze was getting stronger and it was already high tide and still rising three hours before scheduled high water. Soon the house began to shake. Doors started to blow in. The sea piled up and the wind screamed. In fifteen minutes, thirty-four houses on Fort Road were completely swept away and fifteen people were lost. One workman managed to get into the roof of a house as it was set loose and then managed to transfer to a small piece of debris on which he was carried to Osbrook Point clear across the bay. A whole family, the Moores, rode across the bay in a similar fashion in the attic of their house. Meanwhile, in the old fort at the end of Napatree, three men and a girl trod water in a concrete gun emplacement throughout the hurricane. The girl became hysterical, but was supported by the men. At midnight, when the storm and tide had finally slackened, they stumbled back along the completely devastated beach.

Now, on chart 358, you can see the dots marking the sand banks—almost uncovered at low water—that are the remains of the joint between the elongated southern tip of Sandy Point and the curled back horn of Napatree. The cut is sometimes marked with a pair of stakes, but you can see what sort of channel it is from the depths in feet on the chart, from west to east, three, one, two, one, two, five. That middle one is where we hit—and not the first hit, either, for on that we had lifted the rudder and centerboard, and blessed both hoisting gears. When we hit the second time, we had everything up, and it was necessary to send the marines over the side and make them push. The tide was still going out. The slight ebb combined with Jeffery's shoving to move us slowly, grating over the sand, into deeper water. I dragged Jeff aboard, and we sailed on, giving each other superior smiles as if we'd rounded Cape Horn.

We got off easily, but the grounding was enough to remind

me of previous occasions when I hadn't. My first solo grounding was in Portsmouth harbor, in *Caprice*. I remember the way the mast shuddered, the boat changed direction, the boom came over with a thwack, and my yellow oilskin hat, removed from my head, indicated the speed and direction of the tide that was running fast toward the distant cranes of the dockyard. I hauled rapidly on the centerboard tackle, thereby reducing the draft. The boat freed itself from the mud, caught the wind, heeled over, and—with no board and hence no grip—drifted rapidly sideways until it came once more to a muddy halt. I noticed the green fronds of a water plant poking over the gunwale. For ten minutes or so I tried to bring the wind onto the other side of the sail, so as to get blown into deep water. But when at last I managed this, it was too late, the bathtub was empty. I was surrounded by mud and the thin sound of little rivulets trickling down through the mud toward the crabs and cockles. After further consideration, I tried pushing, and discovered that the boat, though small, was too heavy for me to push alone through the noxious element. Muddy, I sat down in the cockpit to wait three hours for the tide to lift me off again.

Of course, I learned quickly. In the few textbooks that touched lightly on the subject, I found such terms as kedging off, shifting the ballast, and final check before abandoning ship. In practice, I found the mud contained old chain, derelict shackles, rusty anchors, lumps of concrete, and jagged soda bottles. I learned that it was better to run aground at low tide or even at half tide than at the top of the flood, when one has as much water as one ever will in which to navigate or drown. I learned the difference between taking the ground in a twelve-foot dinghy and a thirty-five foot, twelve-ton yacht, drawing six feet, called *Fair Breeze*. The skipper of this vessel handed me the helm one evening as we returned to port. He pointed out two marks and muttered, "Keep those two in line and you'll be okay," as he went below to join his wife over a gin and tonic. On that occasion it was the noise that was most startling—a grinding sound as of Panzer tanks moving over a recently oiled and graveled country road. Later, as *Fair Breeze* settled down to a fifty-five degree list, which she kept for several hours, I stood like a mountaineer on the foredeck, watching the owner row his wife the two miles home in the foggy twilight, and putting off the duty of going below to pump the bilges of Gordon's Gin and any seepage from the encroaching tide.

On another occasion I learned that going aground could have its advantages. This was in the wide Delaware estuary, where we were heading out to sea in a large yawl. The wind perked up, and the night became quite wild. Rather than get worn out and wet through on the first night of the cruise, we ducked back into the estuary and headed for a small river mouth on the western shore marked on the chart with the exotic name, Smyrna River. We ran aground before we got more than a hundred yards in. By then, however, we were in sheltered water and the tide had only a foot to fall. We put an anchor out, rigged an awning over the cockpit to keep off the rain, found some antibug stuff to repel the Smyrna mosquitoes, and sat back—tethered physically and mentally, with no urge to do anything but watch the waves rushing up the Delaware, have a pleasant dinner and a perfectly peaceful night.

It is curious what various things people see in boats. One picnic party I took early on to Napatree Point treated the *Billy Ruffian* as a conveyance for getting from a dock in Stonington to the picnic destination, and was chiefly pleased with the boat's ability to run right up onto the beach, so that one could drop down from the foredeck onto dry land—I liked this ability too, especially at Napatree, where the inner beach shelves steeply enough to leave the rudder and skeg in deep water. Peter Tripp and Frank Jo Raymond were aware of different possibilities in the *Billy Ruffian*. We sailed

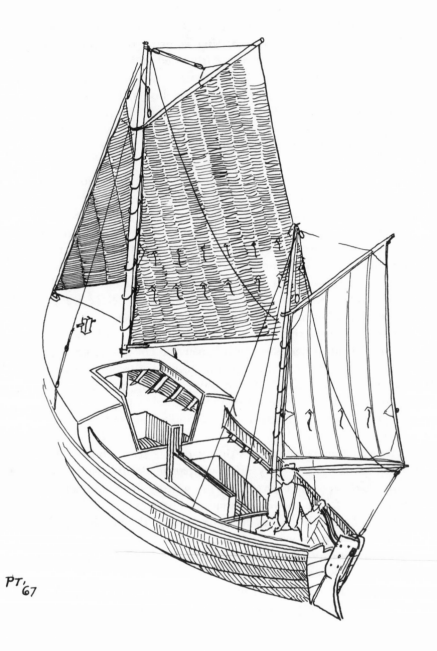

PT'67

out one afternoon round Latimer's Light, which was Frank's old haunt. I contented myself with dueling other boats on a similar course (whose skippers mightn't have known we had a race on), and shouted to my passengers now and then, "Hey, we're taking that Rhodes 27!" and "Look at us shoot past this Ariel!" Peter and Frank nodded half-hearingly. Outstretched on the cockpit seats, their heads tilted up just enough to receive the precious fluid from the bottles of Ringnes they had in hand, they were preoccupied with a discussion of the best ways of reviving a triangular trade between Westerly, Stonington, and Fishers Island. They had no doubt that the *Billy Ruffian* was a perfect boat for carrying cargoes of seed oysters and, possibly, coal.

One day Margot, Liz, Anny, and I took the dory out in a breeze gusting between fifteen and twenty. The *Billy Ruffian* had her lee rail down, her weather chine up, and when we tacked the crew slid down the bridge deck as down a playground slide. Spray made a dark patch in the foot of the blue mainsail. When we finally turned for home, we were soon back in the harbor before the wind. A young man was pumping out his leaky old skiff on a mooring next to ours. As I made my turn, heading into the wind to lose speed and bring our bow to a stop right at the mooring, I could hear the pumping youth say, in Cassandra tones, "Oh-oh." We missed the mooring. We missed the second time, and in falling off to get way again just failed to collide with a nearby yawl. On the third attempt we came up with too much impetus, and though Margot caught the mooring pennant, we were going too fast and she had to let go. On the fourth swing I knew a little more about what sort of way the boat carried and how she reacted in that weight of wind. We made the mooring. By then our neighbor, working off nervous energy, had his skiff pumped dry.

Margot came out with me one morning in thick fog. There is a fine, cocky pleasure in sailing round your own harbor in

fog, while other boats lie at their moorings waiting for it to
burn off (the question is one to occupy people throughout
the day—will it or won't it? The chances are fifty-fifty). As
the dory slides through the opaque anchorage, shapes suddenly appear—bows, masts, and furled sails, names on transoms, mooring buoys, and people in cockpits looking up from
their reading or knitting to see our blue mainsail and strange,
sweeping-sheered craft go by. We sail past people rowing in
search of Dodson's for ice or the morning paper, and fishermen in rented outboard boats, blowing on foghorns and
wondering whether they dared ask which way the head of the
harbor was. It's certainly simple enough to lose your sense of
direction if you haven't a compass and aren't using the wind
—assuming, that is, the wind is blowing fairly steadily
from one direction. We took a long tack across the harbor
until the eel grass off the Wamphassuc shore was showing
beneath the surface. Then we came about and held a straight
course—save for dodging a few rowing boats and moorings—
until the pilings of Longo's Dock loomed ahead, like mega-
liths on the edge of a shrouded land, and behind them piles
of rocks and two old men with bamboo fishpoles. And so on,
zigzagging down harbor from shore to shore. Off the west
breakwater we dropped the mainsail to see how she handled
under jib and mizzen. Then we hoisted the main and dropped
the fore and after sails. Under either rig she seemed well
balanced, though a little less inclined to come neatly about
with the main dropped—having a sail at each end of the boat
and none in the middle seemed to stop her from pivoting
naturally; once or twice Margot had to do some fancy backing of the jib to bring her round.

In late August we day-sailed daily in Fishers Island Sound,
an area which (according to the *U.S. Atlantic Coast Pilot*,
volume 2, "Cape Cod to Sandy Hook"), "has numerous shoals
and lobster trap buoys, and . . . is exceedingly treacherous,
characterized by boulder patches which rise abruptly from

deep water." Currents are fierce, especially for a section that does not have a great rise and fall of tide, and lobster pot buoys are now and then dragged under. The western end is guarded by a set of islets, North Dumpling, South Dumpling, and Flat Hammock, with Seaflower Reef farther out like an advance patrol. Then running eastward down the sound are two irregular lines of shoals, rocks, and underwater obstructions, like the columns of a cathedral forming a nave and two aisles, although in this case the cathedral is not straight but makes a gentle curve. At the eastern end by Latimers Lighthouse, it opens out in a wide chancel, with Stonington on one side, the reefs of Wicopesset on the other, and at the far end, like the choir and altar, Sandy Point and Little Narragansett Bay. Until last year the plentiful nighttime lights marking the various clumps and shoals were unliturgically reminiscent of Times Square, but the Coast and Geodetic Survey have now reordered and abbreviated the lighting system, and it is a little less confusing and a great deal easier to find out where you are. Veterans of the sound on midnight sails have, in time past, found themselves making for Groton Long Point when they believed they were heading for Stonington. In any event, in the *Billy Ruffian* we never worried too much about the rocks we couldn't see. Out of sight, out of mind, at least until the centerboard bumped and had to be rapidly hoisted.

The pilot book is perhaps right in proclaiming the dangers of the sound, but it remains a glorious place to sail. The pilot book is definitely right in describing Fishers Island Sound in chapter 7, "Block Island Sound," rather than in chapter 8, "Long Island Sound." For although Montauk on the eastern tip of Long Island slightly overlaps Stonington to the south, Fishers Island Sound partakes of the swell and the open sea. (Block Island gives its sound its name rather than any protection). In Fishers the summer breezes are salty. Even on calm July afternoons one can successfully whistle for wind. This

is something sailors have just about given up doing in Western Long Island Sound, where the narrow concrete patio of New York City which now stretches half-way out the length of Long Island (the terminal ice-age moraine deposit) raises a barrier of heat that effectively flattens any breeze.

The shore of Connecticut facing Fishers Island is undistinguished in elevation. But in plan, or depth, there are creeks, coves, and small islands. Some of the coves are cut off by bridges carrying the New Haven Shore Line railroad, and you have to poke into them in a skiff or dinghy, giving your oars a quick flip and then bending your elbows as you go under the narrower bridges, ducking your head at high tide beneath the rusty steel girders, and trusting that the Patriot or the Hell Gate doesn't come rattling over at just that moment. There are old oyster beds in some of the coves and often a few swans and ducks. The whole shore is low, and once again well wooded (the early explorers were all taken with the density of the woods), though there are numerous houses, some in clusters of summer colonies, others in settlements like Noank, Mystic, and Stonington. Adrian Block, the Dutch explorer, sailed this coast in 1614, giving his name to the island Verrazano had actually seen ninety-one years before. From several miles out the shore induces no striking feeling—there are no cliffs or headlands. It is a hesitant beginning to a vast continent, giving little indication that the land stretches back three thousand miles to another ocean, rising on the way to snowcapped headlands that make the cliffs of Dover seem insignificant. "The soft green breast of the New World"—and indeed, there is still something to be captured at every landfall of that transitory, enchanted moment Fitzgerald imagined for the first Dutch sailors, seeing a sight that was (though not surely for the last time) commensurate with man's infinite capacity for wonder.

The true coast is probably the continental shelf, buried aeons ago—the drowned shoreline where great canyons mark the ancient mouths of rivers. According to divers' lore, strange ruins have been found. (I have heard one tale, at fourth or fifth hand, about a Navy diver who discovered a masonry tower in twelve fathoms south of Narragansett Bay.) Yet the coast we have now, however unspectacular, is for that very reason good to coast along without trouble or incident, in the right weather and season. I don't mean that you can't get into trouble, for that you can do in the confines of Stonington harbor or in a flat calm in Fishers Island Sound, if you find the tide sweeping you onto the bared teeth of Wicopesset when you haven't got an anchor on board or you have an anchor but the warp is too short. I had to anchor

there one afternoon in *Broomstick* in sixty feet of water. We
would have spent the night there, waiting for a breeze, except that we had some neighbor's children aboard, and we
knew their parents would be anxious. So Russell, aged ten,
waved at an incoming dragger, coming in from a long day of
fishing in Hell Hole, one of the favored fishing grounds off
Block Island. The *Carl J* was owned by one of Russell's
uncles, and she decently stopped to take our line and then
towed us into the harbor at ten knots. *Broomstick* put her
bows up and her tail down and vibrated. I was glad the line
was an inch and a half nylon, that I had taken several turns
around the mast as well as the mooring cleat, and that Mc-
Vitty, who had lent us his boat, was out of town and wouldn't
see us planing in.

The relationship between fishermen and yachtsmen is generally a cool one, like that between farmers and huntsmen
or perhaps even farmers and gardeners. Like huntsmen,
yachtsmen are concerned with thrills and glory, and also,
like gardeners, with neatness and display; whereas the average
fisherman has his mind occupied with the production of fish
and a good market price for them. He isn't, more than once
or twice a year, much bothered about the appearance of his
craft, although in his nautical bones he knows he would like
a trim ship, and he resents the blasted yachtsmen with their
white enamel and scrubbed teak. Yachtsmen, so fishermen
feel, are dilettantes, less serious about the sea. Yachtsmen tend
to feel that fishermen are drudges, their senses blunted by
toil, their appreciation of the element a purely commercial
one.

Some of that August day-sailing I did singlehanded. I
found I had a lot to appreciate in the dory's behavior when
I was alone in her. I found she sailed well with the tiller
lashed with a single line from the weather coaming, while I
prowled around the boat, lounged in the cockpit or stood in
the open hatchway looking nonchalant while powerboats

zoomed up and looked at me in frank wonder. No hands! If I walked down to the lee side she heeled a little more and came up into the wind. If I sat on the windward coaming she sat up straighter and fell off the wind. So I could steer her by putting myself in the right spot. It required, of course, a helmsman's touch to bring her about, which I did near Wico-pesset. Then I lashed the helm again and taking it easy in

the stern quarters, steered home by judicious manipulation of the mizzen sheet.

We made our first cruise on September 1. Here is the log, as I wrote it immediately afterward, lacking polish but preserving, perhaps, the freshness of our adventure.

After Margot and Liz returned from Church and Sunday school, decided today might as well be the day. Gathered gear and junk, all ready by noon, except for Liz, who had disappeared in the direction of the Holy Ghost parade, celebrating the feeding of the starving masses of Portugal by Queen Isabella. Found her at the Portuguese Holy Ghost Club, downing free Portuguese soup. Finally reached the dory, stowed gear, fed other members of the crew.

Made sail at 1:30 P.M. Clear blue sky, not too warm, light breeze. Sailed behind Sandy Point and anchored opposite Elihu Island, south of the channel. Went ashore by dinghy, and Liz, Anny and I walked on the beach prospecting while Margot went clamming on the flat that spreads out to the east of Sandy. Haul, a dozen cherrystones. Margot said she hadn't quite got the clamming technique of the Chipperfield boys, who were searching for clams with their toes, and doing a sort of twist. We went aboard again, retrieved the anchor, drifted aground, pushed off with Yaacov's boathook, and sailed over to the entrance of Wequetequock Cove where we anchored again. I fed Gerber's Tropical Fruit to Anny while Liz and Margot fished, using some of the clams for bait. They caught nothing. Liz kept bringing up her line to see what was on it and kept losing her bait. Lot of waterskiers around. Other boats nearby with men rod-fishing catching fish. At five-thirty we weighed anchor and sailed over to Barn Island game preserve area, ghosting into a little anchorage behind a tree-covered point. The bottom, a clear six feet down, was firm mud—a few shells and underwater plants were visible. The harbor was formed of low, marsh-grass covered banks.

It was a lovely evening. Liz and I went for a sail in the

dinghy for a way up a ditch that drained the marsh, and then made a second trip, with Margot and Anny, who refused to go to sleep, up a wider creek that wound into the woods. We ran fast up this miniature river, our wake lapping the banks. We saw herons, cormorants, duck, and gulls. The sun began to go down over Stonington. We rowed back down our creek until we reached the little harbor which gave us room again to sail.

On the *Billy Ruffian*, Margot cooked her first shipboard meal, while I rigged an awning over the boom. Anny still refused to go off watch, and had a second dinner, this time of minestrone and Dinty Moore stew. (She refused the fried clams, which turned out to be a wise move.) By ten-fifteen Liz and Anny were at last sacked out on the cabin floor in sleeping bags. Margot and I sat in the after-cockpit. A huge yellow moon rose over Osbrook Point, and across the water from Stonington came the sound of revelry at the Holy Ghost. The tide fell, and the dory pointed her nose inland. In the marshes a few birds piped, and overhead we heard the loud buzz of mosquitoes.

Margot and I slept in the main cockpit under the awning, the centerboard case between us like Sir Gawain's sword. We had air mattresses and found it hard to discover the exact point of comfort where the mattress was neither too hard nor too soft. Margot had the last sleeping bag. I had two blankets, an old genoa jib, and a sail bag, into which I stuck my feet.

It was a cold night. Dew fell, and the awning proved to be permeable.

Liz woke at seven.

Anny woke at seven plus ten seconds.

I got up, creaking like a tin man.

Fine clear morning, flat calm.

Margot got up, refused to talk, took four baby aspirins and gave four to me.

It was Labor Day. Margot dressed L and A, while I sorted

blankets, sleeping bags, folded awning and pumped ship. M, heroine, cooked on the gimbaled Sterno stove pan-fried corn-bread, which was delicious with boiled eggs and coffee. Anny crawled into a locker under the bridge deck and had her bottle there.

We were underway at 9 A.M. Light breeze from the south-west. We tacked out of our bay and then swung round Osbrook Point to the Pawcatuck River. We spent the morn-ing on the river, sailing up it with the wind against the tide, and then down with the tide against the wind. We admired the houses at Avondale and the boats on moorings off Paines Yard, and Frank Hall's, and we answered questions from passing yachts: "Say, is that a Chinese junk?" or, somewhat more sophisticated, "Is that a converted Coast Guard rescue boat?" The question was—we thought—better put in Fishers the week before by an Alden Challenger which pursued us across the sound and caught us by East Harbor, coming up to leeward, and deliberately slowing with a great release of genoa sheet—"What is she? She's dandy!" I doffed my beret and yelled out, "A French dory." "Lovely boat!" came the reply, then they cranked on the winches and were away.

Around lunchtime we got to Napatree and anchored in the bay behind the fort. Liz made sand puddings with children from other boats, Anny splashed in the shallows, Margot sketched, and I slept for an hour. When I woke, I felt thick and groggy from the sun, but a hundred feet away across the dunes was the sea and I stumbled over and plunged into a foaming breaker. Soon I had a clear, cool head. We raced home against Charlie and Anne Storrow's Woodpussy, but they made it through the cut, and we, bouncing hard, had to jibe around and go the long way back. It was a slow trip, tide-cheating. Liz and Anny were flat out in the cabin. We turned down the offer of a tow from the senior Dodsons in a Boston Whaler. A Marshall cat-boat passed us at tremendous speed and we hoped she had an engine on, but there was no

sound or sign of it. We made our mooring on the second attempt and I rowed ashore with the gear and then the crew.
Liz, contrary, didn't want to leave the ship. We were all sun-
reddened and strangely enough without colds or coughs. I
took ashore with me at the end of this maiden cruise the
knowledge that I needed a lighter more easily handled anchor,
and also that I needed a compass that didn't, at certain times
of day, acquire a bubble. Home, Margot turned to me: "It
was just awful, but I suppose I liked it."

11

Haze at Napatree

Sailors are sometimes samaritans, saving out of charity, and sometimes salvagers, saving for profit. We found ourselves in a situation in early September that seemed—however indistinctly—to bring out these characteristics. It was once again on Napatree. The weather was suitably opaque, with a haze left over from a thick fog the night before—a haze that a hot, obscured sun never quite burned off. We could just make out the east breakwater from the Point, and when we reached the East Breakwater we could see Napatree; but there was a tangible limit to our vision. We could see so far and no farther.

There was also very little wind. Yaacov stood on the foredeck of the *Billy Ruffian* as we drifted out of the harbor, chanting Arabic wind songs he recalled from his days before the mast on the Levantine trading dhow. We have learned not to scoff at Yaacov's wind songs, since he produced a twenty-five knot westerly that won *White Wing* her class on the first day of one Fall Off-Soundings. After the Arabic chant, he switched to the *Volga Boatmen* in Russian, which, like

the tremendous, moody music in the film *Alexander Nevsky,*
he boomed out toward the Point and the monument marking
its successful defense against the British attackers in 1814.
However, neither the Arabic nor the Russian seemed to influence, on this occasion, the local weather picture. We moved
slowly along behind the breakwater and hovered over the
rocks, well awash in three feet of water, of the reef which
forms a rather treacherous submerged continuation of the
breakwater at its northeastern end. Margot had a fishing line
over the side and wanted to stay there. Yaacov and I made
the majority decision to drift on.

We made it through the cut and anchored in the small bay
formed by the spit curling back on itself. Then we rowed in
and pulled the dinghy onto the beach. Since it was Saturday
afternoon, there were a number of beach buggies and camping trucks, while skindivers were ferreting around offshore,
looking like seals or porpoises in their black wet suits. A
dozen men were surf-casting. At the west end, by the ruins
of the fort, a small crowd had gathered at the edge of the
breakers around a shapeless white object. We stood still and
tried to make out what it was. Then Yaacov said, "Come on—
let's go!" He began to run along the beach, taking heavy
strides in the crepe-soled sandals he insists are good boat
shoes.

The crowd consisted of a family party, two young men in
swimsuits, some teen-agers with a transistor radio, and a pair
of skindivers. A little apart from them on a sandhill sat a
short, elderly, and balding man, and as I glanced at him a
woman wearing a sort of poncho came up the beach and sat
down beside him. Farther along the beach a man and a woman were retrieving what looked like a long piece of teak
from the surf. When they had got it, they brought it over
and added it to a pile of things I now noticed nearby—a life-
jacket, a sail bag, some plastic dinnerware.

What everyone was staring at was a boat. The white shape
we had seen was the doghouse, for the decks were awash, the

hull was underwater, and the mast and boom were floating alongside, still attached by the standing and running rigging. Poking up from the swell were the tops of a group of pilings into which the yacht had chanced and on several of which she had clearly foundered. The swell washed through the smashed doghouse windows. Bow and stern seemed to waggle slightly with the passing of each fortunately not too strenuous sea.

The sight aroused confused feelings: at once how awful and how fascinating. There was nothing "pleasant" in seeing the boat wrecked. It put one quickly in mind of how fast any solid-looking craft could come to a sad end, with perhaps no more reason than a wrong nudge of the tiller to blame. It made one feel that there but for the grace of God went I. And yet, side by side in one's mind ran the appeasing thought, this didn't happen to me, it happened to some other poor fellow, and I wonder what he's doing about salvaging his boat—Has he given up? Maybe it can be saved.

By this time Yaacov had discovered that the balding man and the woman in the poncho were skipper and crew respectively of the stranded yacht. They both looked dazed and aimless, as if they had any number of things to do but didn't know where to start. Yaacov sat next to them and began to question them. I felt embarrassed, and walked down to the water's edge to help retrieve a foam mattress that had just floated in. Yaacov was merely doing what I would have liked to have done, except that I was inhibited by the feeling that if I'd been the skipper I wouldn't have wanted to talk to anyone right then. As it turned out, Yaacov was well-received; apparently they welcomed the chance to explain what had happened to them.

Margot and I asked together as Yaacov came back, "What happened?"

"He's French," Yaacov said.

"I thought he was," said Margot. "Though maybe South American."

"He had bad luck, poor chap," said Yaacov, telling us the story—how the Frenchman had been coming in through Watch Hill Passage the night before, bound from New Bedford to Stonington, when around midnight, in thick fog, he misjudged the current and came to grief here on the tip of the Naps. At first they didn't know it was grief. They hadn't hit very hard. It was calm. But in a few seconds the swell had lifted them up and dropped them down on a piling, which impaled the boat—a three-months old twenty-seven–foot fiberglass sloop with auxiliary engine and four bunks, worth eight or nine thousand dollars, suddenly stuck firm with a small tree trunk rising through the cabin floor and water all around.

After the shock, they were hopeful—it was a clean hole, and they thought if they could get the boat off the piling they might be able to plug the opening and pump her as they got into harbor. But the tide was going down. The boat settled down on the piling, and the swell, nudging the boat back and forth, caused the piling to widen the hole; water came in faster than they could pump it out. Through the fog they could just see the beach, and so they swam ashore, found a camper truck, woke the surprised occupants, and got a ride into Watch Hill village, where they called the Coast Guard, and the owner of the boat. There, in the hotel, they spent the rest of the night.

"Oh, he's not the owner then?"

"No," said Yaacov. "He was just delivering the boat. He's a friend. That's the owner over there pulling that other mattress up the beach. Wearing Madras shorts."

"Oh, that makes it worse."

Yaacov looked puzzled.

I explained, "To run your own boat on the rocks is bad enough, but to run someone else's . . ."

Yaacov nodded, but with no real agreement with this conventional thought.

At first light the owner had arrived from Hartford, and a launch from a local boatyard assisted the owner's and skipper's efforts to recover the yacht. But all they managed to do was cause the mast to fall, the mainsail to tear, and the hole in the bottom to get several feet larger. Later in the morning a workboat belonging to a diving and salvage company attempted to lift the yacht off the piling, but the hoist tackle couldn't take sufficient strain. When we arrived the workboat had just given up and gone home. The owner and a woman who was apparently his wife walked up and sat down by the Frenchman; they all looked exhausted.

"Are you insured?" Yaacov asked.

"Yes," said the owner.

"David," said his wife, "shouldn't you call the agent again?"

"He wasn't in, and wasn't expected back until tonight. We've made the effort. You have to try to save the boat, otherwise they won't pay up."

"You've done that," said Yaacov.

"Yes. Well, maybe I'll try and get through to him again. He's off at his granddaughter's christening."

Everyone dispersed. The owner seemed so calm, and I thought that if it had been me, I would have been hopping mad. We didn't see the Frenchman and his crew again—they were off to take a train to New York. But that evening Yaacov got up from the armchair where he had been half-reading a 1911 edition of Dixon Kemp on *Yachts and Yachting*. Ambling over to knock out the ashes from his pipe into the Franklin fireplace, he said casually,

"What do you say we run over and have a chat with the man who owns the sloop?"

I knew at once which sloop he meant, but I hadn't known that he knew where the man lived.

"He told me he was spending the weekend on Lords Point."

"Well?" I said.

"What have we got to lose?"

"All right." I didn't relish driving around Lords Point, a nearby colony of summer cottages, looking for a man I hardly knew to ask him about the boat he had just lost. But we went. And such is Yaacov's fortune that, driving round a corner in Lords Point, I saw walking along a man called Jim Mooney, a paint salesman whom I had met on several occasions at Hiscox Lumber Company with Smitty. I asked if he knew where a man named David Armstrong was staying.

"Yes," said Mooney, "he's staying with me."

The upshot was that Yaacov acquired permission to salvage the craft if it hadn't already been salvaged. The insurance adjuster was to make his inspection of the wreck on the following morning, and by the time we got there he would have decided what to pay for the vessel. The owner seemed to believe that his boat was a total loss and was adequately covered. So, next morning, Yaacov scurried around borrowing pumps, both gasoline-powered and manual, tarpaulins, pieces of plywood, spare anchors, and warps. He thought it would be possible to cover the hole on the outside with a tarp, strap it fast, and then bung it up from the inside with a piece of plywood—he had flippers and an underwater mask. Once the jury patch was in place, we would pump like mad until the boat was sufficiently buoyant, and then keep pumping while we towed it slowly to a convenient beach in Stonington for more permanent repairs.

The day was a replica of the previous day, hazy, calm, but perhaps a little more breeze from the southwest. We reached out to Napatree, passed the fortifications, and opened up Watch Hill Light. Yaacov was the lookout in the bows. I waited to hear him yell, "She's still there!" or "They've got her beached already," but he said nothing. I looked, and there was nothing to see. The tops of a bunch of pilings showed above the surface a hundred yards inshore. There was nothing on it or near it, no white fiberglass doghouse, no spars floating alongside.

"Closer in, please," Yaacov asked.

We slid toward the shore, making a diagonal approach to which the swell seemed to add its own sidelong motion. We were lifted from one spot and seemingly let fall in another. It made for a slightly helpless, weightless feeling. The tiller didn't react quite normally. I wondered if we were about to be dropped on a rock or piling. I wondered if the boat would manage to work off from the beach when brought into the wind and swell, or if she would slide inexorably up onto the sand.

There were skindivers on the beach. There was also something white—no, several white things—looking like plastic dinghies, or parts of them.

"Do you see them?" yelled Yaacov.

"Yes."

"There must be more. She must have gone to pieces out here."

We cruised around for half an hour, just far enough from the beach to satisfy my apprehension and close enough for Yaacov to feel we were on the spot. We peered over the side and stared into the surface of the swell, the broad bands of blue and green, slices of black, and the blurry reflections of our own faces. We saw shapes and objects, more of them the more we looked, all lifting and changing. But we saw no hull to salvage or anything to do with it.

We sailed back behind the point and anchored out of the swell. Then we rowed ashore and pulled the dinghy up over the mussel-encrusted bank that protects the west side of Napatree. We hastened over the dunes. It was indeed the sloop, or all that was left of it—a piece of the deckhouse, and a section of the cockpit. Yaacov talked to a skindiver and learned that one of their brethren had already salvaged the engine. Armstrong had taken ashore the mast and boom the previous afternoon. We unbolted two cleats from the piece of cockpit; that was our salvage. The sloop had come apart during the night from the action of the swell. There were many smaller pieces of fiberglass scattered on the beach, like pieces of egg shell. Somehow it wasn't much like the wreckage of a ship—there was nothing to sustain the feeling, which even a single splintered plank of wood would have evoked, that something pleasant and useful had once been made of these fragments. The life had gone the moment the shell cracked.

Or so thought I, the proud owner of a twenty-eight–foot ketch-rigged St. Pierre Dory that hadn't yet dared to venture out of her home waters.

The insurance company had agreed to pay for the sloop, and Yaacov, an unsuccessful salvor, salvaged some of his pride by a well-conducted bargain with Armstrong for much of the sloop's gear, buying for a nominal sum the mast (in two fragments), boom, rigging, foam mattresses, and cockpit cushions, the latter being durably damp. Yaacov didn't have a boat, but he intended to have one, and all this would come in useful. Mast and boom reposed in my cellar for several years. For a while Napatree seemed to have lost its allure.

This wasn't quite the end of the matter. I ran into Jim Mooney a few weeks later. He was pottering around in his fishing skiff, and joined us on the steeper western side of Sandy Point, where swimming is excellent in deep, clear water.

"That was all very strange, that wreck," I said.

"Yes, it was no fun."

"But the owner took it pretty well, I thought."

"He's religious," said Mooney. "Which helps."

"Still. One's boat."

"It was his wife who was mad about it. She couldn't get over it, especially since Michel Morel is such a hot sailor."

"Michel Morel?"

"Boy, he was really in a state. He couldn't believe it had happened."

"You don't mean Morel—that wasn't Michel Morel, the skipper?"

"Yes it was."

I had seen Michel Morel once in New York. (The name is not real, but will do.) I had gone to Town Hall to listen to him lecture, and I had talked to him afterward for ten minutes. He had twice sailed singlehanded across the Atlantic, had crossed the Pacific, and had been caught in a typhoon in the China Sea, dismasted, and had survived. His hallucinations had been written up in *Reader's Digest*. His articles were to be read in yachting papers, describing what to do when the water ran out with fifteen days to go. He was a specialist in catching seabirds on the wing and eating them *au nature*. He was a *voyageur*, a man of the sea.

I said, "I know what Morel looks like. I heard him speak."

"Well," said Mooney, with obstinate politeness, "that's what Betty Armstrong said his name was. He's a friend."

"You don't think he was just passing himself off as Morel? I mean, to get the use of the boat."

"Gosh, I don't think so. You must be mistaken."

"You wait and see," I said. It couldn't be Morel.

Mooney dropped by three weeks later, bearing some blue fish he had caught out in the Race. He was closing up his Lords Point cottage and heading back to Springfield, Massachusetts, for the winter. "By the way," he said, at the end of these equinoctial farewells, "about Morel—that was him. I asked Betty."

"It *was*?"

"Yep. He'd lost a good bit of hair, she said—that may have fooled you. And he was in a state of shock. He must have looked quite different."

Mooney went off, sparing me any "I told you so's." Morel there on Napatree—someone I had seen, listened to, briefly met—and I hadn't recognized him. It was a situation that seemed to have a hole in it, through which one could tumble into eternal ambiguity. Why had it happened to him then and there? Why were we spectators? Superficially, the moral of the tale seemed to be that even famous swimmers could drown in two inches of water. It also served—the next time I read Morel in a yachting paper, writing on ocean navigation—to render the author human.

12

Block Island and Vicinity

In September the habitués of the Dodson coffee lounge turn their attention to hurricanes. The memory of 1938 is still gray-green in Stonington. The vision of boats sailing on huge seas into places where no boat (at least in historical times) had ever been, continues to sit fresh but salty in the imaginations of local sailormen, and pushing open the lounge door one is liable to hear the Weather Bureau's current choice in female names almost before the *New York Times* or radio station WNLC has dared to mention it. One September afternoon I walked in to find the fortunes of Dora under discussion—in fact, not only Dora, but Ella as well, for the two ladies were on a converging course. John Dodson Senior (a man who looks and sounds like Humphrey Bogart) had set up on his desk a pegboard chart of the Atlantic seaboard with small black markers to indicate wind directions and the centers of each storm. When they got together Ella and Dora formed a monster hurricane, 150 miles wide, brewing winds of 140 miles per hour. At the moment their joint effort was veering away from Florida and heading up the coast. Would it strike into the Carolinas? Would the high pressure zone move in from the midwest in time to fend the hurricane offshore? Or would it bounce like a pinball up the seaboard and slam into Stonington?

It isn't bad if it isn't the real thing. There is even a charm to a September storm that comes after a long boring stretch of fair weather, like the southeast gale we had last September —a spin-off from Hurricane Faith, which fortunately passed us by way out to sea. There was little activity in the harbor. A yacht or two came scudding in under shortened sail. A yacht that had gone bravely out soon ducked back; she would continue her cruise in a day or so—not that day. Most cruising people went ashore in the Dodson launch and joined anyone they knew in the village round an unseasonable log fire. Gray gusts swept down the harbor, moving the heavily humid gray air. From the deserted club dock one could smell David Johnstone's cigar smoke downwind, as he sat in the cabin of *Chivaree* musing on the polypropylene warp he collected around his propeller during the Fishers Island Race the day before. Charlie Storrow was out on his Starboat, Sam, pumping. It was a day, indeed, for checking the mooring painter and applying fresh chafing gear, and sitting on one's bucking boat, watching a few intrepid fishermen take their outboard skiffs down harbor (the theory being, no doubt, that the fish are all swept inshore on a day of this kind); and it was a day for gratitude that one has a cabin and a large mushroom anchor.

The *Billy Ruffian's* mushroom is four hundred pounds, and in Hurricane Carol, in 1954, it held not only the Lymington Slipway five-tonner that was tethered to it but the forty-six foot ocean-racing yawl *White Mist*, which drifted down and snagged the mooring chain. In Dodson's the veterans consider alternative courses of action. The fishing draggers, says Duke, generally go up the Mystic River, past the Route

One bridge. There is also the Westerly River or West Harbor, Fishers Island, with its well-protected inner cove. "But," says Johnny, "there'll be all those du Pont boats anchored in there ahead of you—you wouldn't want any of that gold to rub off on your topsides, would you?"

McVitty, who has sailed much on Buzzards Bay, recommends Hadley's Harbor if one happens to be in the vicinity. I ask about Block Island. It is all right, they all say, but pretty much as a last resort—waves build up to steep short heights in Great Salt Pond, and the holding ground isn't firm. The island also seems to record the highest wind speeds in any storm in these parts, though that may be because it has a well-fastened anenometer that doesn't—as other recording devices seem to at ninety-eight mph—blow away.

As for the *Billy Ruffian*—the consensus was that if she was in her home port when the blow struck, the best procedure would be to leave her on her mooring, strip off her gear, and let her fill up with rain and sink. The bottom of the harbor was the safest place in a real storm.

We left for Block Island at three o'clock one Monday afternoon in mid-September. Liz and Anny were moored at Mrs. Madeira's for twenty-four hours. Roy Bongartz and his wife Cecilia, who is from London, had joined us for the cruise. They live in Rhode Island and seemed to like the idea of having come into Connecticut to sail to part of Rhode Island again. As we stowed provisions alongside at Dodson's, Roy, a hefty man who sports loud tartan shirts and a Gallic moustache, stood on the end of the dock twirling slowly around and around.

"What are you?" asked Ce.

"A radar scanner," Roy said. "What does it look like?"

He went on being a radar scanner for several minutes. Then, when we'd got things put away, he came and asked sensible questions about the working of the boat.

We outboard-motored out to the east breakwater as we set

jib, main, and mizzen, then fetched out past Napatree in the light southerly breeze. We had the tide with us through Watch Hill Passage. From the lighthouse we set our course of one-thirty degrees and took our departure, not perhaps in the manner ships once did by streaming a log and setting watches for sea, but in the sense of being suddenly aware we were for the first time in our own boat heading offshore out of sight of land. I had spent an hour or so the previous night with charts and parallel rules. I had consulted the tide table and the weather forecast. For although the voyage was merely twenty miles, so that land ahead ought to appear almost the moment land behind disappeared, Block Island was only three miles long. Navigators had often missed Bermuda at the end of a seven hundred mile voyage, and I didn't think it impossible for me to miss Block Island at the end of twenty. It remained a possibility until we got there.

With a fine wind the journey can be made in four hours. In a boat like *Broomstick* you can sail over in the morning, have lunch, and then sail back in the afternoon. For us it was a little different. The light breeze faded out. We rocked gently in the ocean swell, with the buildings of Watch Hill silhouetted on the cliff behind us. Roy told a story about a man he knew who was the last tenant in a New York apartment building. New owners wanted to tear it down so they could put up a bigger and more profitable one. Roy's friend refused to move. The owners removed the light bulbs in the halls. They offered him an apartment in the new building, rent free for a year. They took off the building front door and turned off the water. He didn't budge. They offered him three thousand dollars. He said he was staying put, his lease wasn't up. The telephone company cut off his telephone and he sued them; service was restored. By this time the crane was outside and the wreckers' iron-ball was ready to strike. Winos slept on the stairs and the rats came out to play. He held on. He paid his rent. The managing director of the realty company called him and invited him over to discuss his problem. They offered money, women, psychiatrists.

Roy, who had been lying flat on one of the cockpit seats, sat up. He sniffed the air. "Still no wind, huh?"

"No."

Roy lay down again. He closed his eyes.

"What happened!"

"What? Oh, Earl? He took five grand and the free apartment deal. The moment he walked out the bricks and masonry started to fall. He moved into the new place and on his first night, climbing into the fancy built-in bathtub, he broke a leg. Do you spot Block Island yet, Ce?"

We held a convocation to decide what to do. The afternoon was swiftly coming to a close. Should we turn on the noisy engine and go home? Should we turn it on and go on? We did the latter. The Seagull racketed and smoked, but moved us ahead. Where it moved us to, however, we were no longer sure, since the proximity of the spinning flywheel and magneto housing induced a similar motion in the compass, fixed abaft the mizzen mast a foot or so over the engine. I got out my back-up compass and gave it to Roy, well forward. I had won this instrument as a prize in a regatta on Portsmouth harbor a dozen years before, and before that it had been an RAF fighter-pilot compass. It had a movable grid that one set in the direction one wanted to go, and on whose north mark one then tried to keep the needle pointing steadily. It took some getting used to, but it was a useful second opinion, and just then I hoped that it would do for us what it had once done for Spitfire pilots.

But would it? My trepidation was intense. I wondered when the blasted island would show up. Would we miss it altogether in the dark? Margot cooked dinner on the gimbaled stove—hamburgers, French bread, fried onions, and bilge temperature Norwegian beer. In the twilight I spotted what appeared to be twin islands ahead. Margot said it was a cloud bank. Still, there was nothing else to steer for, and we headed for it, rigging the bicolor running lights to the samson post and lashing a six-volt electric lantern abaft the mizzen as a stern light. A lobster boat surged past us, going the same way, and I restrained the crew from asking which road we had to take to get us where we wanted to go. Soon darkness fell, and I pointed out to Roy the lights of the island—we could make out a fixed red and a white and green flasher, which I told him marked the entrance to Great Salt Pond. I steered for both, and then, when they seemed to diverge, for the flashing—which now funnily enough looked like a rotating—green and white. Two more lobster boats passed, but this time their course seemed to be forty-five degrees different from ours. Roy began to sing the song that dated from his days as a messenger for the American Embassy in Paris:

> Ne pleurez pas, Madame . . .
> Don't cry, Lady,
> I'll buy your bunch of violets,
> Don't cry, Lady,
> I'll buy your pencils too.
> Don't cry, Lady,
> Take off those big dark glasses.
> Hullo, Mother,
> I knew it was you.

This melancholy chant provided a fitting background for the fact that suddenly, after looming strongly overhead, the white and green rotating light had disappeared. I held my course for a few moments. Then the realization of my stupidity came through—high black shadows loomed ahead—and I swung the dory hard round. We were in under the cliffs. The light I had been following was the light of the airport, on the plateau in the middle of the southern half of the island, up over the cliffs. After a minute's consultation with the chart, I found the fixed white light at the end of the breakwater, and once there, lined it up with the flashing red at the inner end. Although it was hot and choking on its own exhaust, the gallant Seagull pushed us along the narrow channel, past the Coast Guard boats sitting at the ready beside the Coast Guard station, and through the gap in the dunes into Great Salt Pond. We moseyed along the shore and anchored in two and a half fathoms close to a dock but out of the way of incoming ferries. We had a drink to celebrate our safe arrival. Then we rigged the awning over the cockpit, hoisted a kerosene anchor light, and—although it was now ten-fifteen—rowed ashore.

It was an enchanting night. We felt the island was ready for our immediate selfish possession. We had got there in our own craft in our own way. The stars shone brightly, houses sat in weird solitude on the edge of fields, and the earth curved up as if to meet the sky. We walked along empty lanes, up and down hills. No one was about. It seemed more like old England than New England—a Yorkshire headland, for instance, or a slice of a Cornish moor. On the top of one hill we saw the airport beacon again, rotating, white, green, white, green, and I thought of the days when wreckers had been as busy here as anywhere on the coast, and no light could be trusted to lead you safely into harbor.

"You know about Silas Mott?" asked Roy.

"No," we said, marching along. "Who was he?"

"Notable Block Islander. He was crossing these moors early one foggy morning when he saw what looked like a man, sitting in a rocking chair with a woman sitting on his lap. 'Must be a hant,' thought Silas—there were plenty of hants here then—and he was dashing away when a voice from the rocking chair yelled out, 'Hey!' It turned out to be Seneca Sprague, and Mrs. Sprague. Silas asked what the devil they were doing, and Seneca explained—they had been spending the evening with the Littlefields. 'He gave us this here rocking chair. It got so heavy carrying it home we both set in it and rested for a spell.' "

We came into a street, sparsely lit, of shops and houses. We passed one of the big white clapboard hotels that date from the island's Victorian heyday as a resort for Rhode Island millworkers. This one was all boarded up, and a lone rocking chair on the empty porch rocked back and forth, back and forth. The Spragues, perhaps. We asked Roy to tell us more.

"Well, there's a local sea serpent, a headless ghost, and a haunted field where oxen used to refuse to plow. Then there's the dancing mortar, an implement made of lignum vitae. Instead of waiting quietly in its pestle for grain to crush, the mad thing used to roll around and hop up and down. They tried fastening it down and using it for a chopping block, to knock the devil out of it. But that didn't work, so they built it into the foundation of a house."

We walked by the old harbor, which is a small haven for fishing boats built behind a breakwater on the east coast of the island, and climbed a rise to our destination, the Ocean View Hotel. Lights shone from a row of windows along the verandah. The old place looked like a set for a Fellini movie, and it seemed appropriate that its bar—laid out in the form of a square with several projections—should be claimed as the longest bar in the world. Half a dozen people were huddled at one point along it: the barman, the manager, the chef, two sports fishermen, and a friend of ours, the hotel's last guest of the season, who was out on the island trying to get some literary work done, and who wasn't at all expecting us. We had a party.

When it burned down last August, the Ocean View had thirty people staying in it, although it had three hundred rooms. We had, however, seen it in daylight during the previous summer (the year after that first nocturnal visit) in the course of the inaugural Block Island Week, when several hundred yachts turned up for six days of racing in the manner of the regatta held annually at Cowes, on the Isle of Wight. There was a day in the middle of that week, which was plagued by either calm or fog, when it blew a gale *and* stayed thick with fog. The Race Committee never lifted its anchor from the mud of Great Salt Pond. We all went exploring instead of racing. Johnny and Tricia Dodson, Margot and I walked around the south end of the island, past the Ocean View—which in daylight we now saw was painted on the front side only; the rear wing had bare wood showing through —and then along the cliffs and beaches. We found one spot that had been in use as the island dump. Old cars had simply been tipped over the cliff, and the engine blocks of Model T's with their cylinders cracked open, and the pistons within rusted and congealed by wind and weather, formed splendid pieces of found sculpture for which we lacked only the lifting tackle and salvage barge. Later that afternoon, when the fog lifted a little, we explored Great Salt Pond. This gave us the opportunity to discover that a Boston Whaler is no canoe when its motor conks out. Using one oar and one piece of board that floated by, we paddled strenuously into the wind, getting nowhere. Fortunately, the skipper of an anchored yacht saw us, and advertised our plight to a passing out-boarder. He towed us for a while and then handed us on to Paule Loring in his modified Block Island boat, *Glory Ann*. Mr. Loring, artist and cartoonist, didn't recognize us as he pulled us to the eastern end of the Pond, though we had met him the year before when sailing the *Billy Ruffian* in Fishers Island Sound, and had matched the two unique craft in a short race (which the *BR* won). The *Glory Ann*, a two-masted cat schooner, was flying her customary signal of good cheer, the British Red Duster, which her skipper claims the right to fly on account of his many friends in the mother country. She looked a craft of great character as she dragged us through the ocean-racing fleet assembled in the Pond.

I might say here that "character boat" is a term that makes

me slightly queasy. It tends to suggest a boat in which eccentricity is the main characteristic, distracting one from other more dubious features, rather in the way the exaggerated moustache of a veteran flier might take one's attention from the fact that he was without one leg, had an arm in a sling, and was blind in one eye. The question is, Can he fly a plane? "Character boats" generally are traditional, one-of-a-

kind creations, built or restored to suit the whims of an individual. And they have single-minded admirers who imagine
that any craft with a fifteen foot bowsprit is a thing of beauty,
and anything with a gaff topsail (although it can't be set in
more than a zephyr and can't be got down at all once the
wind pipes over ten knots) is a real ship. It is a pity that these
addicts of the antique and unusual are often blind to the
beauties of the present. Because ocean-racing, like horse-
racing, is an expensive sport, there is no need to scream
enviously about the dire effects on boats of the CCA handicap
rule. To my mind, some of the most good-looking cruising
yachts of this or any time are the forty-foot sloops and yawls
that Olin Stephens and Philip Rhodes have designed under
the influence, if you like to call it that, of this rule; because
of the general affluence and fashion of racing, there just happens to be a lot of them around, which makes it harder to
judge how elegant they are. Purists who rhapsodize about
old workboats, and snort at the outboard motor as a twentieth-
century source of juvenile delinquency and noisy confusion,
should consider that ultracontemporary outboard-powered
workboat, the Boston Whaler, designed by Ray Hunt. As we
found that afternoon on Great Salt Pond, it doesn't paddle
into a headwind worth a damn (it might have helped if we
had had the oarlocks and oars that are meant to be carried);
but as a fast, capacious, and stable tender, it is unbeatable.
It also has originality, personality, and ability, which are
marks of character. If I had the choice of being adrift in a
storm in an unladen dory or a foam-packed Boston Whaler,
I'd take the Whaler. Though I intend, if I can, to avoid
making the choice.

Two days of racing during that first Block Island Week
stick in my mind. The first day had the sparkle one gets in
mid-summer when there is a hot sun and a good breeze—in
this case a northwester, ten to fifteen knots. We were sailing
a beamy, heavy displacement thirty-two-foot fiberglass sloop—

one of a line of boats that Dodsons were hoping to sell. The first leg of the race was to the northward, from a starting line off the entrance to the Pond. One couldn't quite hold the port tack without running into the beach, and some yachts in our class sailed a long starboard tack and then came about when they could lay the weather mark. We found ourselves with a group of a dozen boats that chose to cling to the beach, taking a short hitch out and then standing in again. There seemed to be more breeze on the beach and some help from the tide. And while the breeze blew, we had an exciting sail— the lee rail down, coming about with the zing of genoa sheets and the rattle of winches, wondering if we could cross ahead of that boat on the starboard tack or whether we should come about under his lee bow. We arrived at the windward mark in good shape and then the breeze dropped and some of the lighter displacement craft eased by.

The wind followed the same pattern during the week, except for the one gale-rent day: brisk at the start, declining thereafter. The first attempt to complete a round-the-island race failed when no boat finished within the time limit. On the second attempt, we reached the north end buoy just as the wind failed and the tide turned against us. We watched the lucky members of the bigger classes, A, B, and some of C, ghost away down the far side of the island, while with the unlucky C boats and our colleagues in D we anchored, after several vain tacks had carried us farther toward Montauk than the direction we wanted. We sat for an hour and a half. We ate lunch. We kept our eyes on a small MORC boat nearby that was fiddling with its anchor chain, we scanned the cloudless horizon for some sign of wind, and we didn't let a minute pass without looking at *Chanteyman*, the famous thirty-two–foot ketch, anchored a quarter of a mile away. She shared our rating. She also had Ed Raymond, sailmaker and skipper of repute, and we felt it an honor to race against him.

At one-thirty it became fairly clear this was going to be

another no-race as far as our class was concerned. The north
reef bell continued to toll dolefully. Many of the boats began
to weigh anchor and motor back down the west shore to
Great Salt Pond. Even if the wind did come, we would have
to average over six knots around the island, which was like
flying. Then, suddenly, the anchor line was standing straight
up and down—the tide had begun to turn. We sneaked it in,
trying hard not to let the twenty boats or so that remained
around us see what we were doing. Then there was the
sheerest suspicion of a breeze—the mainsail took a little shape,
and the clew of the genoa rattled over. There was the merest
tremor in the water behind our rudder.

We had a thirty second jump on that assorted bunch of
boats—a forty-foot yawl, an Invicta, Dolphins, Cutlasses,
Chanteyman, Tritons, Pilots, Arlberg 35s, Vanguards, and
several Islander 32s, sister-ships to our boat. Then they were
all moving in that slowly gathering easterly breeze. It took
us twenty minutes longer to round the bell, our weather
mark, carrying on an absurd race in which there couldn't
possibly be a finish. We were glad that Ed Raymond raced on
too. How we fumed as he slowly gained on us. Tack and tack
we matched him across Cow Cove. He caught us at Old Briton
Rock, but the wind was swinging too, going southeast, then
south, so it was still tack and tack under the cliffs of Clay
Head and down the long expanse of Crescent Beach. It became, for us at least, a match race, and the pair of us seemed
to catch and pass the boats ahead. Sometimes we were close
enough to see the helmsman's face on *Chanteyman*, sitting on
the lee side staring at the genoa luff, serious and intent under
a cotton sunhat. But we didn't wave to one another; we felt
very close as it was. I kept my eyes for the most part fixed on
the small patch on the luff of our genoa, which told me where
I was in regard to the wind. Now and then I had a look at
the water ahead to judge our prospects of wind. *Chanteyman*
took a long tack in to the beach and we gained on him. We

passed, crossing tacks, within ten feet of each other. No sign, no signal. Tense stuff. Then Johnny said excitedly, "Ed Raymond's going way out this time. We'd better come about and cover him." Two other boats were heading out too. But I looked out there and had an impression of flatness and I looked inshore by the Old Harbor, under the Ocean View hotel, and there seemed to be a darker ruffle on the water. So we went in on a long tack and came about to hug the rocks between Old Harbor Point and South-East Point. When we got there and eased sheets for the close reach under Mohegan Bluffs along the south shore of the island we found we were nearly a mile ahead of *Chanteyman*.

That was our victory. The afternoon faded away, and the wind swung into the southwest and faded too. At six-thirty, when our time limit expired, we were making gentle tacks up to South West Point, and we called it quits. Johnny turned the motor on and took the helm for the run up to the Pond. I lay on my back with my eyes closed, the vision of the bright patch of sail in my head superimposed on a kaleidoscopic view of the island shore—the cliffs, the beaches, the hotels, the buoys marking the rocks and wrecks, the grass fields running back from the headlands, sun and shadow, and *Chanteyman*, always there. We were back in harbor in time for dinner and drinks. We pretended to be fed up when we heard that Class A and B boats, starting earlier and catching the tide at the north end, had finished within their time allowances and that one of them had won the round-the-island prize. But in fact silver cups were irrelevant. Our prize was that day.

This burning exposure to the Block Island racing scene was a year and a half distant that night we sat at the longest bar in the world in the Ocean View. Then I had no more idea of the island's shoreline and topography than had been afforded me by my overbrief perusal of the chart and the perceptions of eyes and feet as we marched through the night to the hotel. At 3 A.M. the bar closed. Our literary friend stumbled off down a long, deserted corridor to his corner bedroom overlooking the old harbor. The proprietor shepherded us into the hotel "bus," a ramshackle machine, together with the sports fishermen, one of whom was extraordinarily, though quite nicely, drunk. He called Ce Carol. "Carol," he said. "My name's Bob. It's my birthday."

His friend said, "Bob always gets drunk on his birthday."

Bob said, "Carol's a nice name."

Ce said, "Thanks."

At that moment there was a loud *bang*. The bus shuddered, lurched sideways, and came to a sudden stop. We were at the foot of the hill by the ferry dock, the sports fishermen's craft was nearby, the bus had blown-out a rear tire, and we said—despite the hotel proprietor's insistence on calling a taxi—that we would walk the rest of the way. Ten minutes later we found the pier where we had left the dinghy and rowed to the *Billy Ruffian*. The anchor light had gone out, but dawn didn't seem far away and we left it so. Margot and I slept on air mattresses on the cabin sole (bunks got built the following winter) and Roy and Ce bravely slept in the cockpit under the tarpaulin.

We got up at nine-thirty. I rose and appreciated how Adam must have felt the morning after the Creator abstracted one of his ribs to make Eve. I had slept against one of the oak frames. Roy had a bad case of hay fever. However, our two Eves set to work and made breakfast: grapefruit juice, blueberries, sausages, bread and butter, and Italian coffee. We were underway at 10:30. We motored out of the Pond with main set and off the entrance buoy hoisted jib and mizzen and shut off the power. Sometimes it's nice to have the motor on just so you can glory in the silence or rather the wind and sea sounds when you've turned it off. It was a lovely clear day. We could see the mainland and the water tower at Misquamicut—we aimed a little to the left of it and ignored the compass. The breeze slowly built up during the morning and the *Billy Ruffian* romped along. We saw fishing boats, sport fishermen, a large schooner, and, close at hand, an atomic submarine. We thought we saw a target ship on the far horizon. Ce noted aloud that we were between the ship and the sub. Roy kept a lookout for practice torpedoes, and sneezed, and held his head. We were off the lighthouse on Watch Hill Point at two-fifteen, with the gong buoy to port going through Watch Hill Passage, and the bell buoy to starboard. I was glad it wasn't foggy, because I don't know how good I'd be at telling the difference between the gong and the bell. I thought of the unfortunate Morel, and I thought of another passage that can be tricky—the entrance to the harbor of Rye, in Sussex. The hazards of it have been

described by Hilaire Belloc at his hyperbolic best, with his prejudices working for him rather than—as they sometimes worked—against him.

Any man making Rye Haven must first resign himself to the will of God, and consider, especially if the boat is running and a little over-canvassed, that death is but a mighty transition; that it is all sand hereabouts, with no cruel rocks to tear the tender body with their horrid fangs; that nothing is worth calculating in life, because things happen by fate anyhow, or by chance, but certainly not by our direction; and that if, or when, she strikes, it will not be his fault. There is no man living that can tell you the deep into Rye harbour, for it shifts with every wind, and at the best it is of the narrowest. As for me, I have made it four times in my life, each time I have touched and never have I struck, and how the thing was done no one knows. Nevertheless, they still build ships in Rye, and the tradition of the sea is all about it, though what used to be the old haven is now a field.

13

October

People who have lived on this coast for any length of time are quietly unanimous in liking October best. It is the month —in fact, a six weeks' month, running into early November— of brisk but still warm winds, of days as mellow as the leaves of trees. The hurricane season has passed, and winter gales haven't come. Summer people have gone back to the cities, children are in school, and in the mooring areas of the harbor where some boats have already been plucked out, there is room to maneuver and swing. It is the time of the year for blues fishing, and indeed crowds of boats—all power-boats—are out in the Race in the early morning, like companies of soldiers with mine detectors each worrying a patch of ground. Although in this case they surge forward over the tide and then drift back with it, and show little of the discipline of soldiers—any sign of a fish being landed or even of a rod bending double causes the other boats to break ranks and dash toward the lucky craft that must, they assume, be in fortunate, fish-crowded water.

Early in October Smitty and I decided to see what sort of fishing boat we had in the *William R.* It was a warmish afternoon with a west-southwesterly blowing at fifteen, with perhaps twenty in the gusts. It was also full moon, and we carried full sail out on the full ebb tide through Lords Passage, which (reading from west to east) is the second from the west in the series of five passages between Fishers Island Sound and Block Island Sound. We left Wicopesset Island, which is really just a vicious pile of rocks, well to starboard, so much so that the tide carried us sideways across the reef on the far, eastern side of Lords Passage. Again, the chart was in the cabin, I was trusting Smitty's local knowledge, and Smitty was trusting my assurance that the boat was truly shallow-draft and had never hit a rock. Afterward I saw that there is a spot marked one foot, just east of the red nun that marks the east side of Lords Passage.

The swell was large and steep, though not quite surf. In fact, a pair of skiffs were anchored on the edge of the reef, rising and falling, with fishing lines tautly stretched out. We tried to run along the seaward edge of the shallow ground, but the tide was too strong, and we fore-reached out into clearer water. I was glad there was that much wind, because she handled well in the unsettling lop and seemed to have enough power to cope with the ebb tide, which gave us the constant feeling of having the rug pulled out from under our feet. Smitty had both rods in action. They were propped up over the windward quarter, several feet apart. We reached in through Catumb Passage, between Lords and Sugar Reef, and it felt as if we were traveling fast, as indeed we were through the water, although not over the ground beneath. The ebb was so strong we barely made headway through the passage, which has a wicked spindle-beacon on the starboard hand, marking the rocks—a little farther to the east—of Sugar Reef. The beacon is as dangerous as the rocks. (I have a chart plotting device from a big Chris-Craft that hit it.) Of course, I was doing my best to keep the *Billy Ruffian* headed straight through the passage, and to prevent her from slipping down on the beacon or rocks. But Smitty liked being held there, balanced between wind and tide, with the lines running back with the ebb and the lures running deep—a position which seemed to me immensely precarious. Wasn't the wind, as it always is when you're in fierce tide, much lighter? Weren't we being set down on the spindle?

"That's the stuff?" exclaimed Smitty, with enthusiasm. "Get her in closer to the rocks! That's where the fish are."

I twitched the helm nervously. Fishermen are different. I managed to convince him that he would have us firmly wrapped around the spindle unless he cranked in his lines. We just made it through Catumb, and headed up toward Napatree, where Smitty set me a course through the lobster pot buoys close to the pilings, with the rocks under the fort as a reward for undue leeway.

"Think you can make that?" asked Smitty, letting his lines run again.

"We'll see," I said. But we did, with a little to spare, helped by the counter eddy that here, as under the Portsmouth harbor fortifications, ran along the shore against the ebb.

"This is where the fish are," said Smitty. "They're just in here."

One of the rods began to bend at that moment, and Smitty reeled it in. But it was seaweed. All we caught that afternoon was seaweed and—I thought—a thrilling sail. Smitty agreed, though disappointed that we got no blues. He thought the *Billy Ruffian* was a good fishing boat, with room for improvement in the way of an engine that would control her in the tide.

I went out alone a few days later when it was blowing over twenty from the northwest, to see how the dory handled under jib and jigger in those conditions. It took me several

attempts to learn how to bring her about thus rigged. The
art seemed to lie in sailing her full for a few minutes, gaining
speed, then to swing her round hard and fast like a sailing
dinghy, letting the jib lie aback for a second before releasing
it. (Later I found that she handled better under main alone,
if necessary a reefed-down main, than with jib and mizzen
alone, these being useful steadying and balancing sails but
lacking the mainsail's drive.) Coming back into harbor I had
a few adventures. First the mizzen sheet came adrift—the
block on the clew end lost the lashing that held it to the
boom. The jib sheets were cleated too far away to reach
without jumping forward. So it was hold the tiller down with
one foot to keep her up into the wind, counteracting the
pulling jib, then find a small piece of line (how grateful one
is for little bits of line lying around on these occasions), cut
the frayed end of it so that it could pass through the hole in
the boom, then take several turns through the eye of the
block and round the boom before making fast.

Then, with mizzen trimmed again, a quick jibe to avoid
a dinghy, nearly awash, on a mooring someone had stupidly
planted out in mid-harbor to hold a salvage barge. At which
point the port jib sheet parted, answering the question, may
I use manila sheets in cam-action cleats? The lone mariner
dashed for the high foredeck, holding the flogging sail in one
hand, gripping the cambered deck with his knees and toes,
untangling the snarled and snapping mess of jib sheets with
the other hand, and then tying a reef knot in the severed
parts—conscious, most of the time, that from the fine colonial
houses along the harbor binoculars were being trained on
him, and persons who were waiting to watch the gaudy
sunset were saying, over their martinis, "Whatever is that
young man doing?"

Small white caps were pursuing one another down the
harbor, but a dozen tacks, each a close reach rather than a
beat, brought me to my mooring. I was more than ever grate-

ful that the boats that had been my neighbors all summer had gone. I aimed the *Billy Ruffian* for the antenna pickup and plunged forward, catching the pickup, but neglecting to cast off the jib sheet as I went by. Instead of rounding up into the wind the dory continued to sail. I had to dart back and cast off the sheet. The mooring pennant had begun to strain away. The jib flicked over and knocked off my beret into the water. I said to myself, Don't panic. Make fast the mooring pennant. Down jib and furl on foredeck. Untie dinghy painter from mooring loop. Board dinghy, row downwind after beret, floating inside up, recover it, hardly damp. *Impermeable Foulard.* Reboard vessel. Continue to stow, furl, consider lash-up, ponder methods for making dory a more efficient single-hander.

Singlehanded and long-distance voyagers tend to turn up in Stonington at this time of year—men in crazy, mixed-up catamarans heading hopefully for Florida, or professional captains picking their weather to take a plush yacht south. However, the Hiscocks, in the course of their third circumnavigation of the world in *Wanderer III,* also dropped into Stonington one October, and a young man named Peter Rose, who had just sailed the Atlantic in a twenty-three–foot Thames Bawley—a fat little high-sided, clinker-built gaff cutter, with red-brown sails, rusty rigging, and less room in her cabin than the *Billy Ruffian.* We were out collecting mussels on Napatree the day we saw Rose sail in round Sandy Point and up the Westerly River to Avondale, drifting along with the flood tide that was about to lift the *Billy Ruffian* off the sand where we had grounded her close to the mussel bank. Francis Chichester had sailed his *Gipsy Moth III* through Fishers Island Sound earlier one summer, and when hailed, had accepted our invitation to come in for a drink. He had raced over singlehanded in thirty-three days and was picking his wife and son up in Boston for the trip back to England. Both Chichester and the Hiscocks seemed to be particularly modest people, quietly spoken, courteous in a way that suggested they were perhaps no longer sure of how to deal with people who lived most of their lives on land—or is it that the sea is the great school of manners, where the rough edges of human pride are rubbed smooth? I admired them all, and had not a jot of desire to emulate them.

As for the mussels Margot caught on Napatree: she collected them in our collapsible canvas bucket, and that night, although she had a fever, cooked a superb paella with them. We ascribed the fever at the time to the fact that she had gone mussel-collecting with leaky boots (bought at the local thrift shop for seventy-five cents). But later, when the fever had gone and a stomach sickness had lasted a month, she went for tests at the New York Institute of Tropical Diseases, and the cause of her illness was more directly blamed on the clams she had caught and eaten that first evening of our inaugural cruise. The waters of Little Narragansett Bay, however pretty, are polluted, and the shellfish found in them are unsafe, and will remain so for the next few years until the towns on the river and bay acquire proper sewage treatment plants. (Napatree is washed by continual tide, and its mussels

seem to be germ free.) How a tropical bug gets to Little Narragansett Bay is a question you might think worth asking, but apparently they find it no more difficult to get round the world these days than do lone voyagers.

Another visitor comes at this time of year in greater numbers. The cormorants are to be seen standing in groups on rocks and pilings, drying themselves out with their wings spread and their noses rather haughtily raised; for although they are industrious fishermen, according to Hay and Farb, my authorities on cormorants, they have insufficient oil in their wing feathers to keep the water out, and consequently after several dives they are so waterlogged they can hardly fly. That is why you see them flapping along in such a lumbering way close to the water, making for a good drying-out perch. The early settlers busied themselves clubbing cormorants to death in great numbers, but the birds were protected after 1920, and are now booming again—which should give heart to despairing conservationists. If man makes up his mind to save something, he can.

Stonington is fortunate in already having saved—as a State Game Area—the section of swamp, marsh hammocks, and creeks known as Barn Island, which forms the indented northeastern shore of Little Narragansett Bay. After our overnight cruise there we had meant to go back, and so made a picnic trip on a late October Sunday with some friends, the Brodeurs. It was a bit foggy in the morning, though it burned off a little by noon. Paul Brodeur and I collected the *Billy R* and brought her round to Sea Village to embark the women and children. Then we ran down the channel north of Sandy Point with a gentle breeze. Opposite the mouth of Wequete-quock Cove the breeze dipped, and the fog thickened. We lost sight of Sandy Point and Barn Island. Johnny and Tricia Dodson had been lost out here for several hours without a compass the week before, and after bumping and blundering along the rocky shoreline, they had made it up into Wequetequock, where they hauled the boat ashore in someone's garden and cadged a ride home. I held a course somewhat to the left of the channel leading round Osbrook Point. Paul stood on the bow with the boat hook poised to fend off any threatening rocks. The breeze couldn't have been a better weight for a maneuverable approach—the dory just slipped along. I had the centerboard mostly raised and the rudder hoisted until only a foot remained in the water. We saw the trees first of all, for the fog seemed to be parted by them, and as it was low water, coming into a cove just south of the little bay where we had anchored before, most of the rocks had their gray shoulders well above water. Paul gave several of them a passing nudge. In the middle of the cove I swung the *Billy Ruffian* into the wind, such as it was, and directed her final coasting-in to the mud and marsh grass cliff, eighteen

inches high. The stem plumped in. The bow overhang actually overhung, and first Paul jumped down onto the dry grass with the eight pound Danforth and line, which he dug in twenty-feet inland; then down went children, straw mats, picnic materials, wine, and women. I examined the clear water under the dory and saw a few snails, but since the tide was rising there was no chance of finding her hung up in a little while between two rocks, which is something to bear in mind when gunkholing in tidal waters.

This place where we landed was a miniature coastal plain, twenty yards wide. It ended where—with slightly higher ground—underbrush and stunted wild oak grew in hardy profusion. The little wood surmounted what appeared to be an island, perhaps was "Barn Island" once, though there is no trace of the barn; but in fact was now a peninsula, with water on three sides and marsh, sometimes flooded, on the fourth. We decided to call it Oak Island and the cove Fox Cove. After lunch, we circumambulated the island, finding weathered boards, the top of a coffee table, duck blinds, birds chattering and pirouetting. The fog had lifted altogether and the afternoon was hot and dry. Fishing skiffs were out in the channel, but we had this part of the world to ourselves—a private wilderness, except for a small plane that swooped down to look at us, perhaps because the *Billy Ruffian* looked from the air too large for such shallow water. What is there to do for long in the air, save come down and look at boats? The children crawled through the grass, chewing sticks and picking strange red plastic-like weeds. Paul and I followed a deer run for a little way, and found the spot of crushed grass and gnawed bark where it had bedded down.

We were back in the Barn Island area a week later, this time to explore the farthest northeast creek, which snaked into the marshes for a mile or so. Yaacov stood in the bow as we followed its sinuous course, yelling Port, Easy Starboard, or Steady as rocks showed up just below the surface.

We saw mergansers, brant, and half a dozen swans. A small
earth dam brought us to a halt, and so we tied up to a maple
tree and walked around the pond, whose waters the dam
held back. There was an old skiff beside the pond, with no
paint on it, and—to judge by the way the planks fell away
from the stem—no fastenings in it either. The skiff had had
a purpose there once—small fish were jumping above the
pond's surface, as if to declare their triumph over the long-
departed fisherman. We walked up into the woods, finding a
hill which allowed us to survey the far marshes and the tall
radio aerial high above the wood-shingled roof of the house
of the refuge's part-time warden, Bill Ryan. I haven't been
to see him for several years, but one Christmas I dropped in
to ask if it was all right for me to walk around over the
frozen marshes, and coming back from the walk, Mr. Ryan
invited me in for a cup of coffee, told me about duck, egrets,
and deer, and showed me the big radio transmitter and re-
ceiver with which he would be able to communicate with
ham operators all over the world as soon as he got his license—
he was studying for the test just then. It was curious to think
of someone in that little house stuck on a promontory in
Barn Island talking to people in Tel Aviv and Valparaiso.
Before I left, Mr. Ryan gave me a pheasant from his freezer
for our Christmas table. I came back with a bottle of wine a
few days later, but he wasn't in, and so I left it on his doorstep.

We walked circuitously back to the *Billy Ruffian*, carrying
the small children, stopping every now and then to get our
breath and take it in deep gulps of the salty air, mixed with
the smell of peat that has taken centuries to mature, the odor
of a hundred plants, and the animal life that thrives in the
expanse of grass, mud, and water—a sort of half-way house
between land and sea. The colors of the marsh at this time
of year are a fine gray-green-yellow-brown, overshot with the
red and orange of the woods, and lined with the darker
green-brown meanders of the creeks. There must be some-

thing in a marsh that appeals to our original watery nature. I experience there among the goldenrod, periwinkles, and cordgrass a primordial sense of *dejà vu*. Here, a million years ago, some ancestors of ours must have first crawled from the depths and spent perhaps another million years, all of them happy.

Yaacov and I turned the *Billy Ruffian* round like a barge in a narrow canal, he standing on one bank pushing the stern, I on the other pulling the bow. Then, just before bow and stern swung away, we jumped aboard. The wind that had favored us on the way in, had now swung too, and favored us on the way out, so that we ran in stately fashion down the little creek, surprising the fiddler crabs and sending up a cloud of ducks as we came around a bend.

Mid-November came with thunder and lightning, one of those storms that hovered over the village with bright flashes and loud claps, reminding the Stonington ghosts of the British bombardment of 1814. Harry Mueller's house was hit and the roof set afire. The morning was clear and blue and

crisp, and the season had changed. After lunch I went down to Sea Village where the *Billy Ruffian* was tied up, with the idea of taking off sails and other gear in preparation for laying her up. But in the lee of the Point the sun was warm. I hoisted the sails to dry them while I pumped out the torrents of rain water, and then, with sails up, it seemed silly not to go for a last sail. The jib was already ashore, but I cast off and found that the strong weather helm could be partly counteracted by raising the board and sailing her full. I reached out to the bell off Napatree, jibed round it, and then reached back home. I jibed because she didn't seem inclined to tack with her usual zest, without the jib. (In that sentence you have a fine nautical example of the horrors of English pronunciation—jib is jib but jibed is gybed.)

Out in the southwester off Napatree the air was cold for the first time. When I opened my mouth I swallowed great gulps of chilly wind and my teeth ached. Two Coast Guard helicopters chattered northeast up the shore, where fifty winters ago the Coast Guard surfmen would have made their patrols on foot, and the *Jane Dore*, a sixty-foot schooner-dragger, came in round the outer breakwater with a white bone in her teeth and her tail down, from a hefty November haul of fish. I made a neat landing alongside the Sea Village dock and was grateful for the sun and less wind in the lee of the Point. I dropped the sails, unlashed them from booms and gaffs and then removed these spars from the masts.

14

Thanksgiving

After a week in which the dory reposed at Sea Village, and was gradually divested of gear, the masts unstepped, and the lockers cleaned of the last box of soggy cookies, I chose the day after Thanksgiving to take the *Billy Ruffian* round to the harbor under outboard power and to prepare her for hauling out by the freight house. The previous afternoon, working up an appetite for turkey, my friend Jon Swan and I had worked on the little natural slipway next to Pi Henry's lobster shack. We had moved one menacing boulder and, with the aid of two wooden wire-cable drums, had shifted a pair of long and heavy timbers down the slope to make the "ways" on which we meant to haul her up. We collected what we could find in the way of rollers, which was several sections of three-inch diameter iron pipe. I still didn't have too clearly in mind the procedure I meant to follow, but I thought that with a sturdy three-part block and tackle rigged to the railroad track that passed the head of the slip, we wouldn't find it too hard to haul her out. We motored round in the afternoon, appreciating the winter spar buoys that dotted the harbor and the breath that showed in clouds in front of our faces. It was raw weather, and the short voyage seemed a sufficient duty for the day. Hauling her out would be our job on the morrow. I thought of tying up to a rickety little landing stage, close to the slip and just in front of the Henry clan's venerable sword-fishing boat, the *M-City*. (This craft, plumb-stemmed and fantail-sterned, presumably had another name once, which fell off her stern, leaving only her port of origin—M, or Morehead City, North Carolina, which has served her as a name ever since. Powered with a hefty auto engine, the *M-City* could often be seen steaming into the harbor at the end of a weekend—and if you didn't see her you could easily hear her, throttle wide open, a trail of beer cans in her wake from the sword-fishing grounds off Block Island. Dubbs Henry used to replank her bottom every other year. I believe they caught several swordfish on one trip, but it was a surprise.) In any event, the little landing stage was unreconnoitered, and so we motored on another hundred yards to one of the Dodson finger piers, where we turned the *Billy Ruffian* round so that we would be able to move straight out the following morning—not to waste any of the tide. By this time it was raining hard, but I took a little time to harness the dory between the pier and the pilings, with two lines forward and two aft, so that she was restrained like a prize bull, able to rise and fall with the tide but unable to chafe against the dock. I was a little more finicky about the correct slack and the right hitches than I usually am, for some reason, but Jon bore with me, although the foul-weather gear I had lent him was torn.

When I was satisfied that the *Billy Ruffian* was as happy as she could be between pilings, instead of free to roam around her mooring, we went home to dry out. We lit a fire in the Franklin stove, poured ourselves some therapeutic rum, and encouraged Marianne, Jon's Dutch wife, as she concocted

Nasi Goreng from leftover turkey, rice, and a satchel-full of Indonesian spices brought for the occasion. We toasted each other, and decided that the day after Thanksgiving was one on which thanks could, with equal reason, be given.

From the start, Thanksgiving plus two left us doubtful on this score. I got up at seven-thirty and raised a bedroom window-blind, so that I could look out to Sandy Point and the intervening waters. The view was striking. Gray-white combers were galloping in toward Salt Acres. A thick scud blew over the surface of the water. Waves were breaking all along the southwest shore of Sandy Point, and on the roofs of the houses on School Street and Hancox Street, the television antennae were shaking and waving their sparse aluminum branches. The plan had been that Jon and I would haul the dory at 9 A.M. But I thought a survey trip was first in order, and leaving Jon and his bride abed, I made for Sea Village, where I found my dinghy upside down and half adrift, sand and weed under the foredeck. It wasn't hard, however, to haul it up. The swell was nearly over the top of the dock pilings, and waves splashed at the head of the concrete slip. Dragging the dinghy into the lee of the restaurant, I met a carpenter putting up storm shutters. He said the radio had announced the tide was running five to eight feet above normal, and that the barometer reading was lower than it had been for twenty-one years—that is, since September 21, 1938, when the great hurricane wiped out all of Hancox Street, including the buildings on this site.

Peter Tripp had come down to look at his dory, and to be on the safe side we dollied both dory and dinghy up to the higher ground of School Street. Then we drove down to Dodson's, where conditions were worse. The wind, coming from the southwest, was driving the sea at full force against the western waterfront of the village, and neither Fishers Island nor the inner breakwater seemed to be making much of a hurdle for the sea. Dodson's yard was awash. Mooring

buoys that had been removed for the winter were floating inland, followed by Johnny's khaki-painted duck boat. As Peter and I got out of the car, a small blue and white styrofoam dinghy came hurtling toward us some four feet off the ground, swerved with the gust, and hitting the edge of a storage shed, sliced itself neatly in two.

A storm of wind and sea has a lot in common with a severe fever, in which some things are not seen clearly while others jump out at you with a heightened intensity. Neither mind nor vision seem to have their normal focus. Moreover, what you don't do is because of several factors, physical incapacity, and sheer forgetfulness, and what you get done you do under conditions that make any triumph a momentary thing, hardly appreciated, and making no dent on storm or fever, which haven't in the slightest way decreased. In such a gale you prop the upper half of your body against the wind and move the lower half as well as you can in the required direction. Sometimes the lower half seems to go forward while the top is pushed back. Sometimes in a sudden lull you plunge forward off-balance.

Staggering like a pair of drunks, Peter and I made our way to the finger pier where the *Billy Ruffian* was moored. We paused at the beginning of the dock to take in the spectacle of seas alternately dashing over the dock and squirting up through the planking; the conjunction of forces making a fierce chop. On the inner side of the Travellift pier lay the *Maggie Fury,* a forty-five–foot Alden yawl, her winter cover ripped to shreds and the supporting framework collapsed like so much kindling. Facing directly into the wind and seas, the *Billy Ruffian* was truly bucking, and I saw at once the virtue of her wild shape and sheer—somehow never called forth in calm water; it matched these wild seas. Up and down she bounced, plunging her high prow into the waves but never taking it directly over the stem. The flare parted the waves at both bow and stern. Although she hobbyhorsed violently, the commotion that resulted was far less than it would have been with a boat with less well-balanced lines. The front half of the boat behaved in the same way as the back half, and there were none of the exaggerated reactions one gets from a boat with a fine bow and broad stern. However, there was the danger she might get loose. The steep waves rollicked in and the swell lifted her and dropped her a bare foot from the inshore pilings. My mooring lines now looked extremely frail. But Peter had brought a heavy warp with him, and hanging out over the edge of the pier, with waves splashing up over his knees and the wind flapping his jacket collar against his ears, he managed to toss a loop of the warp over the samson post. Then I led the free end of the warp out to the far end of the pier, as far to windward as I could get it, thus doubling up the lines in the most sensitive quarter.

Up ahead, the sounds of the *M-City*'s engine came diagonally down wind in staccato bursts, and I noticed for the first time that she had been lifted by the extreme tide over the rock seawall—against which I had thought briefly of mooring the afternoon before. Her owners were aboard, trying to get power at the right moment when the swell held her up off the rocks to take her out into the harbor again, but wind and waves pressed her farther in, toward the freight house. Fishing draggers were leaving the exposed southern flanks of Longo's dock and dashing for cover behind the northern pier, where they rafted up in threes and fours. And beyond, in Fishers Island Sound, a thick haze of spray rose fifty feet or so above the surface. But I didn't have time to stand wonderstruck. Johnny was yelling something upwind, words which came to us like those yelled by a child into a tin can pretend-telephone at the end of a piece of string. We dashed for the main dock, where his schooner *White Wing* was moored. This dock pointed straight southwest, and *White Wing* had been neatly aimed head to gale. But now the dock piling to which her bow line had been made fast carried away, sheered off at water level, and her bow swung out away from the dock. Held by two spring lines and a stern line, *White Wing*'s port quarter pivoted and ploughed into the dock—wood chewing at wood. Meanwhile, the springline running forward pulled at a new angle and began to rip its way aft through the winter cover. Before any of the band of watchers—John Dodson Senior, Johnny Junior, Fult, Chester, Peter, or I had a chance to do anything—the rip lengthened. The wind got underneath. Then, with a loud pop, the entire cover peeled off and flipped over the lee side. There was a quick discussion, and then Chester, the yard manager, cut the bow spring line. *White Wing* swung slowly round, her bow pushed by the waves and the wind. Fenders were jammed in between the dock and her stern rail. Johnny jumped aboard with fresh warps, and soon she was moored again, stern to wind, starboard side sprung away from the dock, and her port quarter furnishing ample evidence of what can happen to a vessel in thirty seconds—several days work for a skilled carpenter like Fult to deal with the following week.

Hoarse, exhausted, we took cover behind the plateglass windows of Dodson's store, drank coffee, felt the building shake, and thanked God we weren't out in it. It blew a steady fifty, and several times the wind gauge registered—for a minute at a time—seventy-five. It was what Sir Francis Beaufort (who invented the Beaufort scale) would have termed Force 10—a whole gale. From within the store, it was less a vicarious experience than it was simply a modified experience of the real thing. The windows rattled. Spray ran up and down the glass. When it cleared momentarily, we could see the remaining dinghies on their outhauls between the piers filling up so that only their gunwales showed above water. Gas cans, oars, cushions, fenders, and several pieces of piling banged against the dock end. A flock of gray plastic duck decoys, anchored by tiny lead weights, bobbed above an outboard runabout, of which one could see only the top arc of its white vinyl-covered steering wheel. It was all somewhat surreal. I remembered the seventy-knot gusts that had struck us on the way to Bermuda on my one race there, the water rising above the cabin floor, the seas running at the height of the mizzen mast for twenty-four hours, the clammy lurching horror that was the cabin, the pump clogged with the labels of canned goods, the seasick near-certainty that one was going to die, later on the fear that one wasn't and finally, on the far side of it all, an abstracted feeling of nothing mattering much: the noise of the wind, the pounding of the hull, and the stinging, grinding waves the only reality. It was a good day to be on land.

On the way home I stopped at Frankie Keane's news store

to get the morning paper. The storm had ceased to be of interest there, in what generally serves as the village's exchange for up-to-date news and gossip. However, that was "uptown." Down on the Point section Delinda Cunha told us she'd lost ten shingles off the west side of her roof, and Mary Madeira, our fourteen-year-old babysitter, reported that her family's television antenna was down. Next door, Peter returned to find he'd lost the top three sections of his Franklin stove pipe.

I had an hour's nap after lunch, pooped by the wind. Then Jon and I made a third trip to Dodson's where, at low water (the height of a usual high tide) we bailed the *Billy Ruffian* of a hundred gallons of rain water. The wind still blew. We doubled up the stern lines in case the wind went round from the west, where it then was, to the northwest, and kept blowing for two more days the way northwesters in our parts generally do. Then we went home for tea and rum and played darts, while listening to the wind.

Next morning was relatively calm. It was cold, with a ten-knot breeze, and Jon and I did some more pumping and unshipped the ballast. We got the Seagull going on the second tug of the starting cord, cast off all the warps, and motored her onto our slip as high as she'd go. Peter arrived to assist us, and we sent him off to find something a little more powerful than my Renault for hauling power on the tackle. When he got back, with a car whose owner, for his own comfort, shall remain nameless, Jon and I had the rollers in position. Even so, the big Chevrolet had its work cut out. We had taken a warp right around the dory, so that the pull was transferred to the entire boat rather than to just one point on her. We had to put chocks behind the rear wheels of the car. The slipway was a little too steep, our rollers too thin, our angle of pull not perfect. And the dory didn't like being pulled out—she resisted being dragged from her proper element, and up on land became gawky, ornery, almost intractable, hard to pivot, putting her head up and digging her skeg in—

showing no willingness whatsoever. But by late afternoon the *Billy Ruffian* had been hauled alongside Pi Henry's little lobster shack, was jacked-up on old sleepers and cable spools, waiting only for a tarpaulin to make her completely snug for winter. A few yards away the *M-City* sat where the storm had left her on her rocky ledge; there until spring, said Dubbs Henry cheerfully. Plenty of time then to nail on some new planks and then, on a high spring tide, lever her in. I admired his spirit. At home that night we counted our blessings: the dory was safely out, we had not been shipwrecked, we had had good sailing. It was a second Thanksgiving. Next morning I stayed in bed and, doing as I was told, looked after my suddenly tremendous cold.

15

Winter Quarters

I think the people who dash south when winter comes and continue sailing in warmer waters miss something that has to do with the swing of the seasons, the balance between a time of action and a time of contemplation—of hibernation, if you like, though I hibernate in a study rather than the way my forefathers did in a cave. I don't have to keep putting branches on a fire, for my room is heated with warm air that comes with a barely audible whiffling sound through a duct in the wall. I look out through a window at the snow and the frozen ground on the far side of the harbor. In the afternoons I take a brisk walk around the village, swinging down Main Street past the lumberyard, the railroad, and Dodson's, and passing the *Billy Ruffian* sheltering behind the lobster shack I stop for a moment to tighten up the girth ropes holding her cover down. I knock lumps of loose snow off the foredeck. Ice crests the rocks at the water's edge, and the white-tipped spar buoys lean against small floes. Once or twice a winter Peter and I go for a row. On Christmas afternoons we take one of his small dories over to Sandy Point, to gather firewood or salvage an old skiff that would be better left abandoned, but which we tow home anyway. Sometimes we go beyond Sandy to the edge of the ice which, in February, blocks in Watch Hill and Barn Island. Peter rows bare-handed. Rowing in a calm is preferable to sailing in a nice breeze in this weather, since the wind makes the cold pene-trate, and rowing keeps you glowing warm. Except for a few lobstermen, we have the bay to ourselves.

Some Sunday afternoons I unhibernate altogether and go frostbite racing on the Thames at New London. A fleet of Penguin dinghies is stored there in racks on the Thames Yacht Club beach, and some thirty people turn up to lift them down, polish them diligently, rig them, launch them, and enjoy an hour of fierce competition. When the wind blows steadily over twenty knots we don't sail, or when the tempera-ture is much below twenty degrees. The trouble comes when it's about twenty-five degrees and blowing fifteen, gusting to twenty-five. Those are the afternoons the Boston Whaler crash-boat has a job to fulfill, as the Penguins flounder and

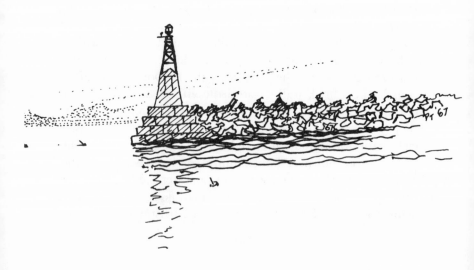

swamp and, now and then, capsize. (The drill is to forget
the boat at first but haul in the sodden pair and whisk them
ashore; then come back and retrieve the boat and any items
of gear found floating at the scene.) Penguins are very sensitive racing dinghies that require a delicate touch on the helm,
and one grows fond of them, perhaps because they are so
demanding. But when the wind is dead astern and strong,
and the water choppy, their behavior is decidedly eccentric.
They want to come up into the wind. A restraining tug on
the tiller causes the stern to roll. The bow consequently digs
in even more, and the boat even more wants to come into the
wind. The pressure on the helm gets harder. The helmsman
tells the crew to shift her unthinking weight aft, quickly, not
too much—only a few inches. Back! But it is too late. The
pressure on the helm has suddenly vanished. The dinghy rolls
to windward, back to leeward, windward—over and under.

"How can you call it fun?" is the standard question. But it
is—the two-minute tension of the starts; the quick tack-split-
ting in the barely noticeable wind shifts; the jockeying for
position that will let you in around a crowded mark or allow you to squat on the lee bow of a competitor, slowing him
down with a skinful of dirty air; and always the chance of
making up lost ground on the final windward stretch to the
finish. We simmer down with a cooperative effort at putting
the boats away, and then take to the coffee and doughnuts in
the clubhouse, where on the worst days there is a log fire.

In February and March the fittest survivors hold on. The
landscape is monochrome: sky, water, houses, and ground so
many shades of gray. My house shakes, and the northwest
wind, gusting to fifty-five, works its way through the cracks
in the clapboards and through the slits where weatherstrip-
ping and mouldings don't quite match. The furnace makes a
continual hum and the oil bill moans. I admit in these weeks
I sometimes weaken. In the Stonington Free Library I seek
out books on the Everglades. McVitty is going to Bequia to

take off the lines of the last whale boats. I borrow his Hachette *Guide Bleu* to the French West Indies and read about the untrodden beaches of St. Barts. The children have flu and Margot has Stoningtonitis, which is largely the product of managing a house full of children with flu when it is ten degrees and blowing and everyone with money is going to Guadeloupe or Bequia. After a dutiful postdinner hour with the works of Ruskin I reach for the November past copy of *Yachting*, with articles on cruising in southern waters, and I open up on the floor in front of the Franklin stove Chart 1002, Atlantic Coast: Straits of Florida and Approaches. *Abaco*—how about Abaco? The unusual name has romance in it. I like the flat names of its settlements—West End, Hopetown—full of incongruous poetry and dark rum. I savor the word mangrove, and think of the keys or cays. Coral comes in twenty-five hundred varieties, and in that area a score of these are at work, secreting lime on lime. "Coral skeletons are attractive," says the *Golden Guide to the Southeast*, "but living coral is even more so."

At this time of year in Stonington the skeletons rattle around in the closets. Women decide to leave their husbands and then exercise their right to change their minds. When two or three people gather together they generally talk about real estate—how old Johnny Souza sold his cottage to a rich divorcée from Greenwich and bought a ranch house in Paw-catuck, but now wishes he was back again; about how much the Thompson house fetched and what will happen if the Plax division of Monsanto, in the old machine shop building, comes to an end; and about how we will all move to Nova Scotia with the coming of the high-speed eastern seaboard train. We relive past glories, like the Halifax Race, and we fight old battles, such as the Battle of Stonington. The reaction to the past trumpeting of local patriots has set in, and a few sophisticated modern observers actually suggest that there was no battle. They propose that the British fleet paid a courtesy call and got fired on by the impetuous defenders of the Point, who claimed a great victory.

Unhappily, this was not the case. One winter I wrote to the British Admiralty, and received from the Admiralty Librarian and the Public Record Office, in return for photostat charges of "£2. 17s. 0d." copies of their records concerning the engagement. Henry Hotham, commodore, reported to his commander in chief that he had ordered Captain Sir Thomas Hardy to make a visitation there in force, since he believed the "Town of Stonington has been conspicuous for preparing and harboring Torpedoes, and giving assistance to the insidious attempts of the Enemy at the destruction of His Majesty's Ships employed off New London." (In fact the torpedoes seem to have been prepared in Norwich, which was too far up the Thames for a visitation. But Stonington was probably chosen as a convenient example.)

The pages of Hardy's log contain evidence that the town was bombarded (though, as Hardy reported to Hotham, "the Houses being constructed of wood, none were seen to fall");

that the shallow-draft brig *Despatch* heroically anchored within pistol shot of the Battery (on the site of Plax), and suffered two killed and twelve wounded, before being forced to withdraw; that several truce parties exchanged visits (during one of which, aboard his ship *Ramillies,* we know that Hardy showed the shore party the couch on which Lord Nelson had died); and that, before dawn on Saturday, August 13, at 3:30 A.M., with light breezes and clear, in company with the *Pactolus, Terror, Nimrod,* and *Despatch,* the *Ramillies* called off the visitation, weighed anchor, and with small boats ahead sounding, stood down Fishers Island Sound. The log reads:

> at 5.30 Grounded off the Northenmost Dumpling Furled sails employed lightening the Ship and carrying out a bower and stream anchor Got the Pactolus's Stream in on our Larbd Bow, and hove a strain to prevent her forging on shore. Boats of the Squadron assisting carrying out Anchor Cables and Hawsers, started 20 Tuns of Water forward got all the Foremost guns Aft, Shot etc.

In the afternoon these lightening measures paid off, and with the small bower anchor laid out astern, the *Ramillies* floated again. Guns and shot were moved forward and things got back to normal. A Stonington truce party came aboard. Next day, the sounding parties found a better passage between the North Dumpling and the mainland. A seaman called James Shelden fell overboard and was drowned. Several small boats were observed making sail out of the Mystic River, and Hardy sent armed boats in pursuit. At 8 P.M. they received aboard from a schooner eight bullocks and twelve sheep. During the night, at anchor in the sound, boats rowed guard around the ships.*

Some winter evenings we meet in the back room of Peter's house, where his wife Mary plays ragtime on the small piano, and Peter with empty bottles, saucepans, dripping faucets,

---

* For a contemporary American account, see Appendix B.

and a hunting horn makes on his tape recorder a gripping drama called *Sea-Monster of Wicopesset.* On other evenings, since man is naturally polygamous, I think about other boats. I think about forty-three–foot schooners that need new fastenings, new garboards, and new love. I ponder sixteen to twenty-foot fast centerboard boats, a little more portable than the *Billy Ruffian* seems to be, in which I could go camping cruising on Albemarle or Lake Champlain. I wonder about the possibilities of a planing barge yacht—a sort of thirty-foot Penguin. But of course I also have long periods when I remain true to the *Billy Ruffian,* and I consider modifications I will make in the spring—foam flotation under the cockpit seats, and a longer, less smoke-creating outboard well.

On quiet winter days when the very air seems frozen you can hear the bell buoy at the east end of Noyes Shoal reminding you that the sea is still there, and that it is never still. Snow lies on the beaches of Sandy Point and Napatree, and Fishers Island and the Dumplings look like butter islands, suspended above the surface of the Sound. But in

March, the longest month, there is wind to spare. The weather changes day by day. Finally the geese fly overhead. Last year it was on March 30, around eight o'clock, just as Margot and I were sitting down to dinner, when we heard the sound of all those klaxon voices. We rushed out into the garden and saw the silhouette of the V, passing over the Point and going north across Little Narragansett Bay, the voices fading.

"Do they keep up that chatter all the way?" I asked aloud.

Margot said, "Maybe they have to keep reporting to each other where they are and that they're all still there."

The event of the geese ought to have been the true harbinger of spring, but the following morning the temperature was in the low twenties, and it felt like winter starting all over again.

16

Second Summer

It was not to emulate Francis Chichester, but rather to arrive in style at some friends for the weekend, that I went
voyaging singlehanded the following summer. We had had
to go away in the spring, and the *Billy Ruffian* was launched
late again. But Johnny Dodson had painted the topsides for
me, with the kindness of a true friend, and getting back I
had the bottom professionally caulked by a man sent over
from Stonington Boat Works; a man whom my witty friends
said had never caulked a seam in his life, but was learning
fast. In any event, she leaked less than she did in her first year.
The dilapidated New Haven freight house had burned down
the month before. Yaacov, who had been moored alongside
Pi's lobster dock in a newly acquired Yugoslav motorsailer,
Haviva, had jumped out of his bunk in the middle of the
night and extinguished the sparks as they flew onto the tarpaulin covering the dory. I helped Johnny launch *Shimmo*,
(the Vineyard Interclub he had bought on selling *White
Wing*) after a midseason refit, and then he picked up the

Billy R with the Travellift and launched her too. It didn't take me long to step the masts, stow the ballast, and put off until the winter the finishing of bunks and lockers in the cuddy. In early September I called my friends in East Hampton, Long Island, and said that since we hadn't found a babysitter and since Margot didn't want to come with the children, I was accepting their invitation alone; expect me Friday night or Saturday morning.

From Stonington to Three Mile Harbor (which is the port of East Hampton) is twenty-four nautical miles sailing as directly as possible; say a six-hour sail with a fair wind and tide. But that direction is southwest from Stonington, and this was the precise point from which the wind was gently blowing as I dropped my mooring at nine-fifteen on Friday morning. Since no sailboat has yet managed to sail directly into the wind, and the *Billy Ruffian* has managed less than many others, I therefore counted on the distance that I would have to sail, if the wind stayed in that vexatious quarter, as being more likely forty miles. I reckoned it so, but I didn't dwell on it, for it was a lovely morning, and I had five hours of tide with me going west, and maybe six if I decided to go through Plum Gut rather than the Race. I had shopped before leaving, and stowed my supplies in the cuddy: Dinty Moore stew, canned peas, instant potatoes, peaches, apples, bread, milk, sugar, and coffee. At Ernie's delicatessen I bought a hot pastrami on rye—a crazy choice, fit for a picnic in Central Park rather than lunch on the wavy deep.

I spent the morning taking long tacks up Fishers Island Sound. The tide just about offset the dory's customary leeway, and by noon we were abreast of New London, crossing the wake of an outbound submarine and just making it across the bows of a tug towing out a barge loaded with sludge and waste—I was glad to be to windward of him. I ate my pastrami sandwich, which by this time was cold and greasy. I opened a bottle of Ringnes beer, took a sip, propped it up while I trimmed the mainsheet, felt the boat bounce on a wave and heard the bottle go over. The wind, a little more in the south, had picked up. The dinghy was cantering along, and a short fountain of water shot now and again up its centerboard trunk, for which I had forgotten to make a plug. I lashed the tiller, let the mizzen run until the dory seemed to be happy to stay on course, and then pulled the dinghy up to the lee quarter. It was the first occasion I'd had to realize that high coamings could have a disadvantage. Leaning over them, they pressed into my pastrami-filled stomach as I held off the dinghy with one hand and bailed it out when the other, and then, grunting, stuffed loops of the dinghy's anchor-line down the centerboard trunk as a sort of baffle system, and then topped this impromptu plug with a life-cushion and the two-pound Danforth on the end of the line.

I came on the starboard tack before Bartlett's Reef and headed out across the Race toward Valiant Rock. I had de-

cided to continue down the Sound to Plum Gut. The New London-Orient Point car ferry, a converted LST, came charging up astern, looked as if it was going to go ahead between me and the reef, and then changed course, going behind and to leeward of the *Billy Ruffian*. I doffed my beret to the skipper, who waved back from his bridge over the trucks and cars. These ferries operate in all seasons but winter, when they don't have enough custom to operate economically—a fact which opponents of the Orient Point-Fishers Island-Watch Hill bridge have used as one of the strong arguments against the structure. Unhappily, experience seems to show that a bridge creates traffic where none existed before, and one has to find other evidence to counter the people who want to drive Long Island potatoes to Rhode Island, and truck Rhode Island potatoes to Long Island. One argument, which I would have thought to be enormously strong, is that the bridge would open what is now a bottle neck, and allow the relatively unspoiled eastern end of the island to be mass-developed, paved with concrete, and quarter-acred allotted like all of Nassau County in the west (you can see why the Long Island developers and construction men wanted the bridge). A further argument is money, for the construction of the bridge over rocks, reefs, turbulent water, and the high-priced land of Fishers Island would cost enormous sums. And finally, the built-up embankments over reefs and shallow water designed to carry a roadway rather than bridge-structures, which would simply span the deeper gaps, would have intensified what are already fierce currents, would have presented severe hazards to the navigation of yachts and ocean-going cargo ships, and—not least—would have given this whole eastern end of the Sound a shut-in feeling—the lack of which serves as a great and exhilarating contrast to other water-bounded areas of the metropolis. I am happy that as I write this the monstrous thing has been shifted, in proposal form, westward down the Sound to Saybrook or Bridgeport, where it may make sense.

I came about once more a quarter of a mile or so ahead
of a yacht that was coming in from the Race. For an hour or
so we took a long port tack diagonally across to the Connecticut shore. The wind was gradually freshening and the *Billy
Ruffian* close-hauled as she was made a fine showing com-
pared to her companion, a forty-foot fiberglass Bounty sloop.
The Bounty came up to leeward several boat lengths away
and hung there, seemingly unable to get by. She was under
full main and working jib, and I shall be honest and say
that as she dipped to the waves she exposed a heavily fouled
bottom. Moreover, her helmsman seemed unable to make up
his mind whether to sail her at thirty-five degrees or sixty
degrees off the wind. One moment he was pinching terribly,
the next he was lurching off to leeward. These maneuvers
may have had some relation to the antics of a crowd of

youngsters who were on the foredeck and around the mast attempting to winch the sag out of the luff of the jib. After a while they gave up and let the jib down altogether. Then they hauled it up again. Then they let it down again. After five minutes during which we dropped the Bounty quickly astern, they bent on a genoa, hoisted it, and sheeted it in. Eureka! I had thought before that she would have gone faster if they had lashed the helm and all gone below decks. Now the genoa was clearly in command. Her helmsman still stood at the wheel, looking proud, as if he were in charge as she creamed by. And now at last he waved to me, and all the children waved, their mortification gone. In ten minutes the Bounty was half a mile ahead and eating up to windward fast.

I began to envy them then. It was a quarter to three. At the Race the tide was already ebbing strongly, and here off Black Point, abeam of Plum Island, it was on the turn. I decided that it was now or never—I would make no further progress to the west with this wind for the next six hours— and so I went about and pointed the bows toward Plum Gut, which is the channel between Orient Point (the end of the northeastern arm of Long Island) and Plum Island, and is the northern entrance to Gardiners Bay, on whose southern shore lay Three Mile Harbor. If we managed to reach the Gut on this tack the tide would carry me through, like a flake of soap going down the drain with the bathwater. But it soon became clear that on that tack I wasn't going to come anywhere near Plum Gut—soon I could scarcely aim the dory's bows at it, and aimed so, she was being pinched and wasn't really sailing; leeway was considerable. The east-bound ebb tide added its force to it. I wondered if I could sneak out through one of the passages between the two is-lands east of Plum Island, say that between Plum and Great Gull, or as a last resort between Great Gull and Little Gull, which was nearly back to the Race. In which case, avoiding the rocks, could I carry the tide southeast across toward Montauk, then tack in to slacker, shallower water in Napeague Bay, and working along the shore, be in Three Mile Harbor by dark? The dark was one of my considerations. The rising wind was another. For I had no desire to be sweeping out toward Montauk and the open sea with night coming on and the possibility of a gale. With a crew I might have given it a second thought. By myself, first thoughts were sufficient.

In late summer, in late afternoon, Gardiners Bay, Plum Gut, the Race, and the short section of Long Island Sound that abuts them, make up what can be a thoroughly unpleasant stretch of water. It may have to do with the shape of the coast or more simply with the effect of Long Island—all those roads and houses warmed by the sun, generating a blast of warm air which seemed to drive down the island and be funneled out from Gardiner's Bay. It is an area where you want your reefing gear in good handy condition, your hatches and gear well-fastened, and the helpful assistance of an auxiliary engine if you want to reach any point in the southwest section of the bay. I have since run into several of these thirty to forty mile per hour afternoon southwesters, one of them accompanied by tornado reports (fortunately the tornados went well inland, leaving us with a mild gale), and I am now more than ever glad that my reaction to my first was prompt. In half an hour the wind had jumped from fifteen to twenty-five, with higher gusts, and although no gale yet it was for me an exceedingly fresh breeze. The dory put her lee rail down and her windward chine scarily high. Now and then in the trough of the swell a wave tip would flip off and splash in over the windward coaming. That also was a brand new thing. The seas were not (as I later found them in Gardiners Bay) short and steep, but they were larger whitecaps than any I had yet faced in the boat. The wind blew with clear-sky vigor, and these powerful combers came toward us from the Long Island shore—the hill of Plum Island with a water tower remaining a solid but distant shape, with the sun behind it. Behind me, as I held on to the swing-

ing tiller and the bucking stern, Connecticut seemed to re-
cede into the afternoon.

Apprehension is what sailing is all about. It is a state in
which you have a number of decisions to make (you believe
quite quickly), and a number of factors to consider in regard
to each decision. Not all of the factors are simple, or as simple as wind and water may be. Pride, for instance—will I
lose face if I turn back now? Other people's feelings—will
my friends be upset if I don't turn up? Where will I be able
to make a phone call to tell Margot I'm all right and to tell
my hosts that I won't be in East Hampton this evening after
all? If I don't make it today, shall I have a shot at it tomorrow? In which case, where would be the best place to spend
the night so that I can make a good start in the morning?
Somewhere behind me—Niantic Bay—or back on Fishers Island—Hay Harbor or West Harbor? Or am I being chicken?
Perhaps I should carry on for an hour or two and see where
I am then. The wind may shift or falter, and I certainly do
want to reach East Hampton and pose as a notable mariner.
Meanwhile the dory is hurdling the waves, the jib and mizzen are pulling hard and the main, with its sheet let out until
the sail is mostly aback, flaps loudly. The clew end of the
boom dips into the waves. Spray flies up into the center of
the sail, making a dark blue patch. And everything splashes
and creaks and hums.

A little after four, I eased the jib and mizzen sheets and
put up the helm. I was being sensible. I would run back to
West Harbor for the night. The decision was weighty, and
I failed to think of another, complementary decision that
should have been made. Right then and there in mid-sound
I should have reduced sail—reefed the main, or taken in jib
and mizzen. As it was, the apprehension continued. I had a
wild ride.

It is nine miles from the spot off Plum Island where I had
a change of heart and course, at four-ten, to the spot by the
Dumplings, off Fishers Island, where I arrived at ten past

five. Allowing for a little more than a knot of favoring tide, and for a minute or two of imprecision in my measurements, the *Billy Ruffian* still made that run at roughly eight knots, which for a twenty-eight–foot dory ketch is going some. But in those following seas I was appreciative of her "doryness," of her double-ended lines and her high, flared tombstone stern that seemed to cause the quartering sea to curl off and twist away. In one lull I lashed the tiller, slackened the main so that the boom went right against the lee shroud, and then I hauled up the centerboard most of the way. Thus trimmed the helm was light, except in the worst gusts, when she tried to round up into the wind and had to be held firmly back. It was blowing harder than ever, you could tell, because the wind didn't feel lighter as it should have done, running with it; it felt just as strong. The sharpness had gone from the sky and a thick haze obscured the horizon on all sides. No land was visible. Much of the time the dory was surfing, putting her bows down on the steep front of the wave and then, as the wave finally passed under her, lifting them and coasting along on two-thirds of her waterline. Once or twice there was a sharp tug astern. When I took a moment to look, I saw with a sudden drop of my stomach that the dinghy was half-full of water, was swinging wildly along the crests of the waves, dashing way out to leeward and then, at the end of her manila tether, being snapped back in again. There would be a jerk felt through the dory, and the sudden change of the dinghy's course caused the water in her to lurch forward, depressing her pram bow. Once I thought she was going straight down. But the bow was broad and buoyant, and at last I had the sense to realize that I should let out more line, which I did, so that she rode farther back on the seas. Her load of water seemed to settle more comfortably aft. I added the dinghy to the points for continuous reference in getting safely to West Harbor—wind direction, wave height, rigging, sails, visibility, and compass heading.

I was steering just about due east, erring a little to the

north to counteract the tide that was setting out south-easterly through the Race. It was a surprise to see what in my nervous, exhilirated condition I took to be the big bell buoy marking Valiant Rock—was I that far south? I put the helm up a bit to go well north of the buoy, although this nearly brought the dory by the lee. Then I saw that this mark wasn't swinging around like a buoy. It was standing still—it was a trellis tower, with a concrete base—Bartlett's! I snatched a look at the chart and the chart showed rocks and three feet just north of the tower. That was where I was heading. I put the helm hard down. It was now a question of getting close-hauled enough to weather it to the south, and at once it was clear that it was going to be touch and go whether we went slicing crabwise into the tower. The crunch and crack of wood filled my head as I jumped forward and dropped the board. It seemed a long few seconds then, but the centerboard took a grip on the water and we got by with a boat-length to spare.

The remainder of the voyage was swift. The dinghy was still with me and still a preoccupation. A gilt-edged eighty-foot-motor yacht complete with miniature smokestack came rolling by with half a dozen passengers at the tall saloon windows, gazing out at the mad adventurer in his crazy boat towing his water-logged tender. I stood erect at my tiller in my orange foul-weather gear and tried to look properly nonchalant. We reached up the channel between South Dumpling and Fishers Island to Hawks Nest Point, grateful at last to be in the lee of the island. Then it was hard on the wind for the last leg up the harbor, several quick tacks, and a bounce with the centerboard where I carried on too long to the western shore. The wind whistled out of the harbor in black gusts. Moorings were to the right by the yacht club and the power station. I bore left and found a deserted spot at the entrance to the little southeastern cove. I spun the *Billy Ruffian* into the wind fifty feet from the shore and flung over the anchor in ten feet of water, with room to swing.

I would like to say it was an uneventful evening, but that wouldn't quite be true. First, having furled sails and bailed the dinghy, I rowed into the dock and called Stonington. I gave Margot a suitably abbreviated account of my odyssey so far, and asked her to phone East Hampton and explain my nonarrival. Eventually I gave up the phone to a gentleman who had just landed from a large dark-blue power yacht, and who was waiting patiently for me to finish. On

the way out I saw the yacht's name, *Dauntless of Tarrytown,*
and realized that I had just relinquished the phone to
Laurance Rockefeller. It was very nice to know that a man
who presumably had six phones on his office desk and a
ship-to-shore radio phone on his yacht had come ashore like
me to put a dime in the coin box.

At I rowed back to the *Billy Ruffian,* a dark gray cloud
filled in from the west. I climbed aboard just as the squall
hit and rain fell. Fifteen minutes later, as I was appreciating
the fact that I wasn't out on the high seas of the Race or
the Sound, the wind went even farther round, and through
the night came from the north, the exposed side of West
Harbor, and turned my protected little anchorage into a
choppy spot. Still, I had raised the collapsible doghouse
(which I had had made by a convertible-top firm in a mews
in South Kensington, London, of white vinyl and aluminum
tubing), and thus had six foot of protected headroom. Then,
having rigged the anchor light, I cooked dinner on the gim-
balled Sterno stove while the thunder and lightning hovered
around and the classical music on WQXR via my transistor
radio direction finder competed with the static. Although the
restless dory tacked around her mooring, she didn't seem inclined to leave the harbor. At one point I woke during the
night and checked the anchor line. The stars had appeared.
The wind had gone down, and a hundred yards away an
anchor light flickered on a yacht that had come in unseen
after us in the dark.

17

West Harbor

Next morning I was up and off early, faced with the northerly again—a good wind for Three Mile Harbor. But I knew that it would persist from the north for least another day, and if I went there I would have a job getting back. To go cruising singlehanded you need no home or work or wife or conscience. So I spent the morning battling back toward Stonington, against the tide that had helped me the day before, and into an ever-strengthening northeasterly. In the lee of Masons Island, by Seal Rocks, I anchored to tie in a reef and have an unheeled drink of beer. Home for a late lunch I answered questions about my "cruise" with modest remarks to indicate that wind and tide hadn't altogether served, but that I had learned some indispensable lessons about my craft.

That incomplete trip left me curious about the waters westward of Plum Island and also about West Harbor itself. A week or so later, we took the opportunity of a daylong babysitter and the presence of some friends, Yale and Dougie Lewis, to satisfy our curiosity about West Harbor.

The weather was all that it hadn't been before. A steady and moderate warm breeze blew from the south. We reached down the sound to Noank, which was being visited by the *Emma C. Berry*, a coasting schooner built there in 1866, and after admiring the tops of her spars and her broad transom (which was all that was visible round the pilings of Singer's Shipyard), we hardened up for the beat across to West Harbor. On the way we considered old schooners, which were as common in their time as big interstate trucks are today—perhaps someone should think about preserving a Mack tractor and Freuhauf trailer for future generations. And passing Ram Island, where the docks of an unkempt "boat-tel" seem to underline the ramshackle abandon of the place, we talked of the days, only seventy or eighty years ago, when the big packet steamers of the Fall River line or the Stonington line stopped there. A twenty-four–room hotel stood on the island and it had a reputation as a flourishing if somewhat racy summer resort. In 1870 to avoid stringent New York state laws, the light-heavyweight boxing championship of the country between Billy Edwards and Sam Collyer was held there. After forty-one rounds of "bloody battle," Edwards won. Today you can picnic on the island and, not knowing of this, fail to imagine that anyone ever found the slightest practical use for the spot.

In West Harbor we tacked among the boats on their moorings. The big du Pont ketch *Barlovento* was there, and alongside the club dock we could see the tall brass funnel, allegedly gold-plated to save polishing, of the du Pont launch *Maid of Honor*, which was originally brought over from England to serve as the tender for one of Sopwith's *Endeavours*, challenger for America's Cup. Her steam engine has since been replaced by a diesel. We anchored where I had anchored before, off the entrance to the little cove and creek that lead off to the southeast, and after a prosperous picnic of cheese, salami, bread, and wine, we took turns in the sailing dinghy exploring that and the larger even more sinuous western branch of the harbor. There were houses half-hidden up among the trees, some places where the owners clearly enjoyed the admirable arrangement of having their boats moored at their front doorstep, and other places where such familiarity had bred something like contempt—old skiffs, lobster boats, and even an ancient ferry lay half-sunk at decrepit docks. But we weren't prepared to condemn this variety. Indeed, it struck us as a good thing that Fishers Island wasn't all one way or the other.

After a while we got ourselves to the Yacht Club dock and walked along the well-tarred road—more like a private drive than something looked after by a highway department—which led us into the further network of drives and scattered shops and houses that constitutes the village of West Harbor. In the drug store we had sodas and ice-cream (Margot had a hot fudge sundae), and nodded with the forbearance of strangers as the proprietor declared his fondness for the chances a storekeeper gets for looking at young women, and his un-dying animosity for Stonington lobstermen, who, he said, had been tacitly allowed to fish in a section of New York state lobstering territory, but nevertheless preferred to poach in the West Harbor men's areas. The proprietor had been a lobstermen but had quit after all his pots had been stolen, although—don't worry—he knew the Stonington s.o.b. who had done it and he was going to catch up with him yet. We said we didn't know much about that, but we did think Stonington lobstermen were a bit short-changed by the anti-quated state boundaries that carved up the neighboring waters, and we could understand how a Stonington lobster-man might decide—in his zeal to stay clear of the New York conservation agents' helicopters and patrol boats—to become a bit of a New Yorker himself, even to having New York plates on his car and his lobsterboat registered in a New York town that was a hundred miles from the sea..

For a place that is the last of the last great resorts, Fishers Island manages to keep very much to itself, and only the telephone book with its Roosevelts, Lorillards, Whitneys, and such other families of vast northeastern fortunes as the Lifesaver Nobles and the mattress Simmons, indicates to the casual visitor just what is there, in the medieval chateaux whose lawns seem to merge with the golf course, and the resolutely modern villas that sit above their private bays and solitary beaches. Robert Moses would have had fun trying to build his bridge across the island. Small planes land and take off without benefit of publicity, and the big yachts sail to their moorings in West Harbor, and only once in a while is the veil partly lifted. There was a story in the *New York Times* last year that emphasized the island's value in the eyes at least of those who know it. The story dealt with an international financier, Leon I. Ross, who had been deported from Nassau, and who had fled to Toronto with a $2.5 million U.S. tax judgment hanging over him. Referred to as "a man of mystery," Mr. Ross had only one tangible asset in the United States, according to federal agents, and that was fifteen acres of waterfront property on Fishers Island.

One of these summers I mean to go over there and walk around the island, taking a few days to get properly clued-in. In the meantime my feeling about the place is very much affected by a day we spent there not long ago. It was a racing rather than a cruising day—a day with a dramatic center rather than the diffuse, picaresque sensation you have when simply jaunting around in a boat. I was part of the team the Stonington club sent to defend the Parson's Trophy, a silver tea tray, against Fishers Island and Watch Hill. We got dressed up, arrived in a fast launch, did our best not to let our hosts get us drunk before the race at a fine lunch, and then—perhaps we should have drunk more—lost the trophy anyway, and somehow it didn't matter an awful lot, because it was a splendid afternoon spent trying to master the Fishers Island Bullseyes and the tide around the Dumplings, and afterward we had cocktails on the lawn of the club and finally piled back into the launch. We had to go. See you next year.

But on the way out we had to drop someone off at a visiting yawl, and as we approached it Gray Morgan said, "Oh look, isn't that the Imperial Poonah burgee at the masthead?"

I knew the name. It came back as out of the far past. Before I got on board I was thinking of whom I would see, and there, in the cockpit, was a plump figure, holding a tall bourbon and water, wearing a tiny German station-master's cap, the founding nabob of the Imperial Poonah Y.C., Reginald Bennett, M.P. I reintroduced myself. "You'll hardly remember me."

It had been Cowes Week, the best and worst week of my fourteenth year. Reggie Bennett was then as now a psychiatrist and Member of Parliament for Fareham, and, lacking a crew for the Dragon he had borrowed, heard of me, a keen young sailor, the son of a friend of a friend. It was an initiation. We lived aboard Dr. Bennett's sixty-foot Brixham trawler, which was like a railroad flat down below. Daily we raced the borrowed Dragon, *Valhalla*. I was co-crew with Mrs. Bennett, and for the first time came in contact with genoas, spinnakers, sheet winches, and the temperament of a racing skipper. I was shocked at his language as we came around the leeward mark with the spinnaker in the water, the pole wrapped up in the jib sheets, the genoa half up and the winch handle lost in the bilges—and for good measure the Prince in *Bluebottle* going through to weather of us. I wept. At the end of the race, Dr. Bennett opened several bottles of beer, and although I didn't much like what was my first taste of it, I swallowed half a bottle before it was taken away. (Yet nowadays when Margot turns to me, the skipper, after a keen Penguin race and says tearfully, "You were just horrible—I hate you," I find it hard to know what she is talking about. Landsman Jekyll and Captain Hyde.) Back on board the trawler we lived well, though the variety of drink was not immense—for some reason the bilges of the vessel, which had just returned from a trip to Cherbourg, were filled with bottles of Crème de Menthe—so we had Crème de Menthe on the rocks, or Crème de Menthe with soda before dinner and straight Crème de Menthe afterward.

One blustery afternoon I went for a demonstration sail with Uffa Fox in his new Flying Twenty and as the junior member of the party was allowed to sit in the bottom bailing out the waves that broke over us as we planed along at fifteen knots. In some of the races *Valhalla* did quite well. On the last day of the week in very light weather we were ghosting up to the finish line in second place, with *Bluebottle* (skippered by a naval officer that day) just astern on our weather quarter. It was simply a matter of sitting tight, hoping our wind held, and we had it made. Then there appeared running down from windward a naval whaler, three sails set. With uncanny skill it seemed to find the exact line the wind had been following to us, to turn on it, and come down toward us like some slow-moving infernal machine, effectively blocking what wind there had been.

"You goddamn naval idiots!" yelled Reggie Bennett as *Valhalla* came to a halt and the sails flapped. "Can't you see we're racing!"

"Sorry, sir," came a voice from the blank-faced crew of the whaler, whose helmsman—as if now realizing the situation—adjusted his tiller to pass to leeward of *Bluebottle*, leaving her wind undisturbed. Indeed, by the time we had recovered the wind and built up momentum again she had swept by us, and took the second place gun by twenty yards.

"Fancy this," said Reggie Bennett, as we sat in the yawl's cockpit and various kind ladies plied us with drinks and macadamian nuts. "What a funny thing. And what are you doing here?"

I explained that these were almost home waters. I lived in Stonington, and had just spent the afternoon dropping spinnakers in the water and letting the Fishers Island team go through to weather of me—although they were unaided by allied, blanketing craft. I asked, "And how about you?"

"Oh, I came from an afternoon session of the House, attended a board meeting, flew to Deauville, raced Dragons the next morning in the Coupe Etienne de Ganay, got a train to Orly, flew to New York, had dinner in Manhattan, visited our Western hemisphere Revolted Colonies branch of the Imperial Poonah in Oyster Bay, and then with my friends sailed up here. Have to get back day after tomorrow."

West Harbor has these cosmopolitan possibilities, but the afternoon we were there with the *Billy Ruffian* and Yale and Dougie Lewis we didn't avail ourselves of them, or they of us. Just before five we set out again and fetched down the Sound with the full ebb. Yale had just finished four years in the Navy, the last two of them as communications officer on a submarine, and all this abovewater stuff was brand new and wonderful to him. I must say that if I had to go to sea for any length of time I would take a submariner for crew—they are good at making do with a small confined place and at being cheerful in almost every condition. (Later that week in a houseful of tempestuous children, Yale demonstrated great ability both in keeping the children happy and, when he wanted to, in becoming just about invisible.) The wind fell light by Latimers and came into the northeast as we slowly worked across the ebb toward the outer breakwater. Then we thought, why go in? It was a fine evening, the babysitter's bill was going to be split two ways, and the children would keep. I clamped on the Seagull, pulled the starting cord, and off we chugged in the direction of Napatree and anchored within the curve of the snail- and mussel-encrusted bank. We left the mizzen hoisted so the dory pointed toward the beach and what was left of the wind, though now and then a gentle nudge from the swell caused her to ride forward on her anchor line. We swam, and standing in half-a-fathom of warm water washed the topsides. For a beginning to dinner we had onion soup and pilot biscuits, and then while the casserole was warming we rowed ashore, had a painful few yards of barefoot work over the snails and mussels, and then a cautious twilight stroll on Napatree's poison-ivy and tick-infested paths. A small rabbit squatted on one of them. We climbed the gloomy fortifications and picked some wild flowers. On board again, we found the casserole a trifle singed but highly edible. The dark came down, the stars came out. We rigged the running lights and motored homeward, steering for the car headlights on Stonington Point. We found the mooring and made it on the first attempt, although to do so we had to bother Yale, who was sitting on the foredeck hugging his wife with the tender ardor of a mariner home from a long voyage at sea. *Quanta bella giovinezza, qui si fuga tuta via*—how beautiful is youth, and how soon it flies.

NEW LONDON DAY

PT '67

18

A Week on the Lower Connecticut

The Dutch merchant-explorer Adrian Block first sailed up the Connecticut River in his ship *Onrust* in 1614. I set out late one Wednesday afternoon, in early June, to do the same. I spent the first night in Mumford Cove (almost directly across the sound from West Harbor), where I anchored in front of a chic housing development, and watched the planes landing at Trumbull airport. The night sky was lit up by the lights of Groton shopping plaza. Then I ran with the dawn next morning before a brisk easterly, a perfect wind for heading westward up the sail-deserted Sound. I stood on the port jibe over toward Plum Gut, so that the wind wasn't dead astern, and then I jibed over to starboard on a course for Saybrook bar. It was a very different day from that on which I'd made my Plum Gut attempt the year before—the easterly wind was cold, and the sea was gray. But it was certainly a good wind for going where I was going and with the flood tide under her, the *Billy Ruffian* romped along. Though the bolt in the main gooseneck failed off Rocky Neck, and had to be replaced with a lash-up, we soon dashed on, skipping over Saybrook bar, as with all appendages half-hoisted, we disdained the ship channel between the breakwaters and headed upstream on a broad reach, past Griswold Point and the marsh flats of Great Island, past Sodom and Gibraltar Rocks, toward the New York, New Haven and Hartford Railroad Bridge, which had now been in my thoughts for some time and was marked on the chart as BASCULE BRIDGE. Hor. Cl. 139 feet. Vert. Cl. 19 feet (at mean low water).

Connecticut is a word taken from Indian sounds first rendered as *Quinatucquet,* which apparently meant "at the long estuary"—the lower thirty miles or so of the four hundred and one mile river that rises near the Canadian border in Vermont. It is a part of the river where tides flood and the current runs—faster with the ebb tide—between three hundred foot high wooded hills, where there are hamlets and small towns, inhabited by poets and insurance men, and at whose mouth (unusual for so great a river) there is no large city, perhaps because in prehistoric times the river emptied into the sea where New Haven is now, and at the end of the last Ice Age changed its course through a gap in the hills east of Middletown and swooshed past what are now Portland, Higganum, Haddam, Hadlyme, Chester, Deep River, Essex, Lyme, and Saybrook. At which point most people who have written about the river find it obligatory to quote the Hartford poet, Joel Barlow (1787), "Nor drinks the sea a lovelier wave than thine"—a sentiment one imagines to have been truer then than now, when it is inadvisable to take a mouthful of river water, and every spring the long estuary is littered with thousands of dead fish in what is called a fish kill. Even so, "the hills rise grandly, but yet gently rounded and wooded eminences, like the highlands of the Hudson above Anthony's Nose and the Danderburg, and broadening lake-like spaces alternating with narrows. The islets scarcely rise above the water's edge. Upon them trees grow in lovely groves. . . .

Here and there sturdy precipices of granite rise from the water, as at Joshua's Rock. Peninsulas jut out into the river, from whose summits there are superb views up and down. Even the villages that seek its shores stand respectfully aside." That is from the *Boston Transcript*, 1817, but it would still do today.

Coming up the first few miles of the long estuary, I thought about the less than nineteen-foot clearance under the bridge, the twenty-three foot height of my mainmast, the insweeping two knots of tide, the unrigged outboard, and the anchor, which I had at the stern made fast to its line and ready for letting go, if need be, at the river's edge. I considered telephoned information I had received from friends at Chester, that the bridge was usually left open "in season" except when trains were expected. Now, of course, it was shut and a freight train of approximately a hundred cars was rumbling over it. The freight train gone, the bridge remained closed. Another train? No bridge tender onduty? Closed for repairs? The *Billy Ruffian* dashed toward the bascule span, which didn't budge. I put down the helm, came about, and for ten minutes executed a series of delaying maneuvers that must have looked comic to an observer, if indeed there were one. The bridge tender's cabin looked shabby and unoccupied. At last, making a final sally, I blew three petulant blasts on my tin fog horn. There was an instantaneous siren in reply. The bridge went up. I had been let in.

After the Bascule Bridge, the Baldwin Bridge, carrying the Connecticut Turnpike high above the river, was a lesser obstacle. The tide surged around its concrete piers. The main river channel forked left and I took the right-hand branch inside Calves Island, a marsh of mud and grass, and under the wooded Lyme banks. The wind did strange things there in the lee of the hill. Sometimes it blew on the nose, sometimes on the beam, or right ear. Now and then a wisp came flickering from astern. But most of the time it stayed in the tops of the trees, and only momentum and the tide carried the dory along. We passed precariously close to yachts swinging at their moorings—characterful ketches and schooners, with original sheers, bold transoms, scrubbed teak decks, and names—like *Galatea* and *Arabella*—that bespoke affection. The creek narrowed and passed under steep cliffs. Then it opened again in the expanse of Lord Cove, which is set amid marsh islands beneath the slopes of Lord Hill. I anchored there in thirteen feet of water. A squadron of twenty swans cruised away. I had lunch, and then a long nap to make up for rising early. At three o'clock I set out for a row around Goose Island. It lay between the cove and the river proper,

PETER TRIPP '67

joined at the upper end by a shallow channel through which I slowly made my exit, prodding the mud with an oar. On the river side, I had to pull downstream against the full force of tide and the wind, still from the southeast and raising small white-caps. I kept as close to the island as possible—in other words, about an oar's length away; for if one got closer, and one oar was pulling in water and the other was pulling in mud, the latter gained more purchase and spun the boat. I made fast the dinghy to a float at the Old Lyme marina behind Calves Island. Having asked the way to the village, I followed the directions I had been given and found myself not in the village but in a neocolonial drive-in shopping center: bank, package store, and A & P. Still, nothing ventured, nothing won. I bought ice cream and coffee cake and then dashed back to the boat before the fudge ripple could melt away in the sun.

In the late afternoon the weather forecast promised a warmer day to follow with winds continuing from the southeast, twenty to twenty-five knots. Small swallows with peach-colored breasts strafed the marsh, and a white columned Greek Revival house was just visible through the trees. The wind swung the boat contrary to the tide and she rode up over her anchor warp. Downstream I could make out the shapes of piggy-back trucks crossing the not quite symmetrical arc of Baldwin Bridge, while upstream were the hills above Hamburg. All around, the silence of the creek, which wasn't entirely a silence, but rather a soft confusion of distant boat engines, bird sounds, marsh noises, and the tick of the dory's chronometer, a three dollar and twenty-five cent watch, hung on the cabin bulkhead and wound nightly. By eight-thirty the wind had dropped to a point where the fiercest gusts were no longer penetrating the trees on the east bank. Streamers of grass and weed drifted by rapidly a few inches below the surface. At eight-fifty, ten minutes after sunset, my view of Lord Cove presented itself as a memorandum of the kind Turner used to make for future paintings. From bottom to top:

the black rail of the *Billy Ruffian*
a width of mackerel water
a streak of pink water
a thin dash of gunmetal water
a line of silver blue water
then the hills, a bumpy silhouette of black/green/dark gray
above them, pink
fading into hazy orange
fading into robin's egg blue
getting darker and darker in the vault overhead.

What I thought was the light of a plane over Essex turned out to be a star—the movement I had ascribed to it belonged to the boat. Down below in the cabin, kerosene lamps were alight. The smell of kerosene. I sat and wrote to Johnny Dodson, who had emigrated to Australia where he was building fiberglass boats.

Thursday: Lord Cove is fed by Lord Creek, which winds itself into a maze like the channels of the inner ear. I spent three hours of the early morning exploring it, running aground, kedging off with dinghy and anchor, making reconnaissances down uncharted alleys, sounding the depths with an oar: two feet, one foot, six inches, grass. Swallows and swans and solitude. Lord Creek has the strange open quality of a marsh, quite different from the character of the other coves and creeks I ventured into from the river on this and other days. On Chapman Pond, for instance, a small yellow house sits in the underbrush and poison-ivy at the water's edge. You see it facing you as you enter the pond by an overgrown, branch-infested shallow passageway from the river—I rowed in the dinghy. Crossing the pond, you see there are no sashes in the window frames. The house has a bright green roof and a miniature red-brick chimney smack in the middle of it. Within, through the empty shadows, you can make out as in the interior of a doll's house the exaggerated pattern of old wallpaper and a door, which looks painted on. The house sits under the overhanging eminence of Poplar Hill. Did Chapman live here? Did he come by boat?

Selden Creek leads north to Selden Cove and then out to the river again through a shallow side passage, thus turning Selden's Neck (which is now a splendid state park) into an island. I was surprised to find at the entrance to the creek two battered McAllister Towing Company lighters from New York, laden with fishing gear, old stovepipes, and two 1947 Chevrolet sedans. A pair of tracked amphibious vehicles, resembling World War I tanks, were moored or parked on the foreshore. That day they remained a mystery, but they didn't quite block access into the creek, which forms a meandering by-way to the river itself—a backcountry long-way-round. Cliffs and trees overhang the river, and you get the feeling that crocodiles might slither down the dense banks. Busy watching the creek waters for snags and obstructions, I ran the dory's mainmast into a tree hanging overhead and brought down a shower of twigs and leaves. Then as I was clearing up the debris I heard a whine as of an approaching jet. Suddenly a flat gray scow appeared around a bend, bow high and planing fast. Standing behind his vibrating steering wheel, the driver saw my nearly immobile dory in the nick of time, considered with a twitch of the helm passing me on the left, noticed the overhanging rockface into which his scow might slide, and in the last instant clipped his wheel sharply the other way and slithered past with a foot to spare. The driver was grinning like Lucifer, and his two women passengers gave me nervous, where-did-you-come-from stares. The vehicle was a Connecticut River shad boat powered by a forty-five horsepower Johnson.

"On the river, the wind usually blows straight up or

down," Taber de Forest told me that night at Chester. He meant, of course, not that it blew in a vertical direction but that it most frequently blew along it, either inland or toward the sea—and somehow, despite the law of averages, less frequently than half the time in the direction a sailing man wanted to go. I became used to the hard-pressed sound of my outboard. However, even running at half-thrust, with something bunged up in the carburetor, the Seagull got the *Billy Ruffian* into Hamburg Cove on Thursday noon, when sail alone would not. Fierce Patagonian williwaws were blasting from the north down-river, leading me to expect the relief of a beam wind when I turned right into the channel leading to Hamburg Cove. The channel is dredged to a depth of twelve feet and has thick mud close at hand on both sides. But there was no relief. As I rounded the black can buoy marking the channel entrance, the williwaws changed direction too: they came rushing to meet me out of the Cove. I had to bear off, jibe, and try again, and hit the mud, and raise the board, and come into the wind to let past a yacht that had been patiently watching my antics while waiting to power out through the channel. Then I anchored, furled sail, started the old stinker, and thundered slowly in.

On a mid-week day in early summer, Hamburg is a rare place. Deep water in the cove, and not a sign of commerce, of gas, ice, and food, to mar the encircling trees. It is a snug spot in which to ride out a storm, and many local yachtsmen from Essex and Saybrook have put down permanent hurricane moorings for just that reason. I crossed the cove, passed three anchored ocean-voyagers (to judge by the lifelines and baggy-wrinkles) and followed the parade of neat marker posts up Eight Mile River to the Inner Cove. It was a matter of forsaking known beauty for lesser known charm. On one shore of the inner cove were the wharves of two small boatyards. Obscured by trees on the slopes behind were two country stores, one of which turned out to sell postcards and

PT '67

the *Wall Street Journal,* while the other furnished the whole
line of S. S. Pierce provisions, leaving in little doubt the
prosperous nature of the hinterland. I anchored in a few
feet of water outside the area of mooring posts. I could see

the river, now little more than a stream, vanishing round a bend of trees, and hear the cows on a Swiss-looking hillside farm, that hadn't yet been bought up or restored, and thus had the untampered-with, authentic aura of working life—which no doubt puts it in even greater danger of being "done-up."

At 6:30 P.M., having had a nap at Hamburg (the river seemed to make me sleepy at mid-day) and having gone through Selden Creek and Cove on my way up-river, I anchored off the de Forests' house near Chester. To be exact, I followed Taber de Forest's directions and anchored opposite river marker 38a, and then looked for the house, which I finally spotted up in the trees. The house has several slices of river view rather than a total panorama; this seemed to be the way most of the well-considered river houses treated the landscape.

Friday: Overlooking the river, and with a small harbor off it in which they keep a thirty-five–foot bugeye ketch, the de Forests do not take the river for granted. Water is something they care about intensely. "In the industrial parts of Megalopolis," writes the French geographer Jean Gottman, "water pollution has been and still is heavy, and this depletes fish food and reduces the oxygen content of the water." The de Forests' dredged-out little basin was full of dead fish floating on their sides, with heads and tails tipped under water. There have been no salmon runs on the Connecticut since 1857. The shad, however, have made a better adjustment, and this season had been a good one, at least until May 20, when there was a thunderstorm and the shad abruptly stopped running. A good season in this case meant that the gill netters took a hundred thousand fish and rod fishermen landed another sixty-five thousand. A fair night's work was two hundred shad for a fisherman, and three hundred was dandy.

At the de Forests' I also learned about the shabby lighters and amphibious vehicles moored off Selden's Neck. They were owned, it seemed, by "the C & F Corporation," which was a mysterious firm from either New York or Hartford which was thought to have been seeking either salvage, trash fish, or commercial sand—in fact, trash fish; for the salvage was an incidental and not particularly welcome haul, being whatever got tangled in the huge two thousand foot long seine net when the Amtracs tried to arc it across the river. C & F had hoped to catch a hundred tons of fish a day and deliver it by barge to a fish-meal company on Long Island. But river currents were swift and the nets unwieldy. The trash fishermen caught two and a half barge loads, two of which were delivered while the half was buried on "an uninhabited island in the river." What they also caught was a controversy. River people said the operation was unsightly, hazardous, and dangerous to shad and sport fish. The lighters weren't pretty, and the unmuffled Curtis aircraft engines that powered the Amtracs were noisy. It was a bit of a change from the river flowing silently as usual between the green hills. However, game wardens were stationed on the barges to make sure shad got thrown back in, and the shad fishermen themselves seemed to welcome the venture. They thought a thorough spring clearance of trash fish from the river would leave more room, food, and oxygen for the shad.

As for me, I washed my dishes in river water but rinsed them in fresh water from the ship's supply. (I filled my plastic containers and took showers at the de Forests' house, which had kindly been lent me as a base.) Seen in the white enamel basin I use for washing dishes, Connecticut river water is light brown, as if a coffee pot had just been emptied in it. It is very soft water, which increases its industrial value, and upstream such tributaries as the Farmington, Williams, and Ottauquechee pour in raw sewage and industrially polluted water. Some towns on the river have treatment plants;

some do not. The law prohibits people from fouling the river, but until now the law has been haphazardly enforced. Such clamming areas as those at the mouth of the Black River in Old Lyme have been closed. Another sort of pollution is thermal—the Hartford Electric Light Company, for instance, pours into the river some twelve million gallons per hour of water eighteen degrees hotter than the normal river water. The hot water kills the bacteria that would ordinarily destroy sewage. The higher temperature also kills fish. The nuclear power plant of the Connecticut Yankee Company at Haddam Neck will put into the river twenty-two million gallons per hour at twenty-three degrees higher temperature. A study of the effects of this are apparently being made, and one hopes the State Water Resources Commission has the power and the will to force remedial action if the effects are bad. At the moment, no authority seems able to force the power companies to put their transmission lines underground. Connecticut Yankee had lines dangling between the hills across the broad pastoral reaches of the Salmon River, behind Haddam Neck. HELCO has lines across the Connecticut just below Middletown. Lines under the rivers would undoubtedly cost more, though when considered in terms of the great return on investment made by utility companies, or (as the cost would no doubt get shared) when meted out to users at a fraction of cent per kilowatt hour, the cost is small and worth it.

I spent the early afternoon helping Taber load his bugeye *Cicada* for a weekend cruise round to New London to see the annual Harvard-Yale crew race. Then I went back aboard the *Billy Ruffian* and looked through some of the material Mrs. de Forest had given me about the river. There are Committees, Commissions, and Conferences. There are plans for National Parks and—the ever-present automobile— plans for a riverside parkway. The Army Engineers have projects and improvements in mind. There are more and more people, quite a few of whom want to build a house with a view or put up a small dock with a gas company sign. Ads in the *Wall Street Journal* offer "55 Acres . . . zoned heavy industry . . . in heart of atomic power basin . . . will build to suit." Of course, there was industry once before. Shipyards flourished along the river from Saybrook to Windsor and particularly at Haddam, but apart from the difference between wooden ships and heavy industry, there was space then; the river didn't suggest, as it does today, that we have only a single chance to do the right thing.

I read, before dousing the lights that night, *The New Era,* the excellent local weekly paper published in Deep River. Fifty years ago in *The New Era*:

> The shad fishing season closed. The season has not been a good one.
> Addison Chapman of Millington had an ox drop dead Thursday in front of the residence of Wilbur J. Tracy on Town Street.

And seventy-five years ago, in 1890:

> Moodus beat Hamburg, 22-8
> The three masted schooner *Louis Bucki,* built in Middle Haddam in 1881, burned at sea while on a voyage from New York to Florida.
> The stone cutters of the quarry down the river have been on strike this week.
> Miss Fanny La Place returned from a winter's stay in Florida.

Saturday: During the night the anchor dragged—the wake of an oil lighter rocked us loose, and I woke in the morning to find the coffee pot knocked over and the rudder bouncing on the foreshore. It was low tide, and I quickly hauled the dory off into deeper water. Weekend motorboats began to go by downstream, and on Selden's Neck canoes were drawn up on the beach and tents were being rigged. The river once again is becoming a route to and from the interior, with recreation rather than commerce as the purpose.

It was a theatrical day—hot, with a humid breeze, and thick haze rising from the woods. Margot came over for the weekend, and we sailed down river toward Gillette Castle, which looked from a distance like one of those crenellated, pennanted towers that peek through distant trees in medieval paintings. At closer range, it was more like one of those mock castles on the Rhine that turn out to be homes for retired railway men. We anchored off the ferry-slip, making certain the dory wasn't in the way of the *Selden III*, which plies its trade on the now two-hundred-year-old ferry service between Chester and Hadlyme, carrying cars for a quarter and passengers for a nickel. We left the dinghy tied to a ramshackle dock where shad boats were moored. We walked past half a dozen fine old houses, one of which used to belong to the classical scholar Edith Hamilton, and then climbed the steep hill to the castle—an actor's house if there ever was one. The garden and ground floor rooms with ubiquitous glass frogs. Heavily mullioned windows, with tiny panes set in thick mouldings that obscured the superb view. The rooms on the small side, and oddly shaped, with massive light switches and levers to open hidden closets and sliding doors. Javanese straw mats on the walls, and a gallery of bad turn-of-the-century paintings. The library, better stocked, was rather deficient in Conan Doyle. After all, Gillette was an actor who had become famous playing the part of Sherlock Holmes. The de Forests had suggested I ask to see Mr. Mugglestone, the chief guard and an expert in the sliding doors. In the garden I was told that Mr. Mugglestone was in the tower. In the tower, I was told that Mugglestone was in the garden. Perhaps there was a secret stair.

We sailed up river in the late afternoon, ghosting between Lord Island and Rich Island, past Eddy Rock and a row of summer cottages. A man hastened down the garden of one of them, rang a bell to attract our attention, and called out across the water, "Very nice boat!" We waved our thanks for his very nice greeting. On the opposite river bank below East Haddam, light planes were landing and taking off from a small airstrip. We tied up at the dock beneath the Opera House. This splendid piece of Victoriana, built in 1877 by William Goodspeed, shipbuilder, merchant, and impressario, is six stories high on the river side and four on the land and

was rescued several years ago from a sad fate as a State Highway Garage and restored to something like its original splendor. "The boxes, the hanging horseshoe balcony suspended only by slender rods, the proscenium—all featured gold-leafed rococo designs with delicately painted medallions of women's heads spaced at intervals on the forward face of the balcony. . . . The scenery had to be especially constructed on a slant, for the stage sloped upward toward the back, in the Italian manner, so the audience could see the actors' feet at all times." The original drop curtain displayed a portrait of the Goodspeed flagship, *State of New York,* which ran between Hartford and New York City and finally ran aground and partly sunk off her base in Haddam in 1881. The Goodspeed line continued to operate on the Connecticut until 1931.

Margot and I had dinner in Goodspeed's Restaurant, in a long room with Victorian wallpaper, a fountain, and big overhead fans slowly stirring the warm evening air. We saw the musical, *Man of La Mancha,* which was based on Don Quixote, and there brand new and about to go down to New York for a long run. The Sigmund Romberg-crossed-with-Kurt Weill music didn't quite do justice to its rather moving, melancholy theme, which was that the pursuit of an ideal—even a silly one—ennobled the pursuer; but it did succeed in taking us a long way from East Haddam. It was strange to walk down the steps from the theater and board our boat, and then, under main alone, drop silently down the river in the dark to our anchorage off the de Forests. It was a hot and heavy night. The sky had clouded over and thunder growled closer. Just in time we got the anchor down, furled the sail, rigged the tarpaulin over the main boom, and put in the hatch slides. The storm seemed to hover between the hills lining the river, and when the rain began, it came downstream in bands a few hundred feet apart, sizzling on the water. The thunder roared and rumbled hungrily, and the lightning, arcing across the river, illuminated the silver rain, the black sheen of mud at the bank, and the wet, dark-green trees. Tide-rode, the *Billy Ruffian* was swept from astern by the rain which splattered over the hatch slides under the cover of the folding hood. I sponged and mopped as I admired the storm. In his *Voyage of the Beagle,* Darwin noted while on the river Plate that thunderstorms were very common near the mouths of great rivers. "Is it not possible that the mixture of large bodies of fresh and salt water may disturb the electrical equilibrium?"

Sunday: The morning came clear. I pumped the ship of rainwater and cleaned the decks of a squadron of drowned mosquitoes while Margot sliced the melon and made coffee. Then I showed her Selden Creek and Hamburg Cove, but both were already tenanted and for me at least less charming. Sunday is motor-boating day on the Connecticut. Power cruisers saving gas ran downriver at half-speed, making twice the wake they make when planing. The wind vanished from our slatting sails. Because it was Sunday there were all manner of experts about as we drifted into the Inner Cove at Hamburg. Old codgers were varnishing the spars of catboats, elderly gentlemen were sitting in deckchairs by their Lincoln Continentals parked on the grass, and yachtsmen were contentedly fiddling on their precisely moored yachts. I followed the course I had followed on Thursday, past the landing, leaving to one side the line of marker posts and mooring pilings, and headed for the open pool beneath the hillside farm. There was a sudden barrage of warning and counsel.

"Hey young feller, watch those markers!"

"You can't get through there—a big pile of gravel!"

"If you anchor there, you'll be high and dry in half an hour!"

"Watch out your anchor don't drag. It's in mud way deep!"

It was difficult not to feel self-righteous as—navigating on my previously acquired knowledge of the spot—I ignored the advice, paid no attention to the markers, and failed to hit the gravel, drag anchor, or go high and dry. Not that it would have mattered to a flat-bottomed boat that wasn't going anywhere until the same state of the tide next morning.

We had cocktails and dinner in Lyme. First a swimming pool on a hill above Lord Cove (the sort of place and people I hadn't imagined when I was down in the cove below), where there were insurance men, New York lady editors, European photographers, and—as if to stiffen the bunch—a retired naval man who'd run away to sea on a Finnish square-rigged ship at the age of ten. I talked to a young architect who said that Lyme was very much on the defensive against the present exploding wave of the city and people, and was taking such conventional—even obsolete—means of opposition as two-acre zoning. "A Greenwich real-estate man with a few million to spend and a sharp lawyer could overthrow Lyme zoning in a day or two." The owner of the pool by which we were standing, drinking, had done all his own masonry work, and was rightly proud of it. Unfortunately, he'd found after finishing the pool that he didn't own the land he'd built it on, and the rightful owner, who had kept a discreet silence until he saw the project was completed, was able to hold up the amateur mason for a frightful sum.

Monday: Once a year I manage to get up willingly at five in the morning. I was singlehanded again, for Margot had gone back to Stonington the night before. A layer of mist some ten feet deep was rolling across the Inner Cove, and as I motored out through the Lower Cove, now almost empty of boats, the sweet-sour smell of skunk drifted across the water. I anchored opposite Eustasia Island and cleaned the Seagull's carburetor, but this didn't seem to make much difference to the outboard's performance, which remained surly.

Taber de Forest had offered me the use of his fast launch. This was a home-designed and home-made affair of quarter-inch plywood over plywood bulkheads and longitudinal stringers, powered by an eighteen horsepower Evinrude and with the appearance of a miniature long, lean, between-the-wars torpedo boat. At Chester I exchanged craft for the day and slithered up to Middletown at twenty knots. When the thrills of water hot-rodding had quickly faded, I took comparably greater interest in my surroundings as they passed: the fine hop, skip, and jump iron bridge at East Haddam; the shallow, water-lily covered opening reach of the Salmon River; and the construction site of the Connecticut Yankee Atomic Power Plant. Here on the foreshore below the hill on Haddam Neck two tall cranes loomed like the necks of dinosaurs. Half a dozen signs forbade me to land, and so I trolled slowly by, impressed by the huge arches and giant, shadowed vaults of the unfinished concrete structure, which loomed like a piece of space-age sculpture on the river bank. It was a novel interruption. But what it might produce was indicated at the Narrows just below Middletown. There the Hartford Electric Light Company's plant was pouring its golden, murderous hot water into the river, while power lines drooped from bank to bank, even at a height of eighty feet giving one instinctive cause to duck as one passed beneath them—*Scylla* and *Charybdis*.

Although I hadn't intended to go farther, Middletown would probably have stopped me anyway. In both a geographical and emotional sense the long estuary halts there. The lower Connecticut has been called the least exploited natural resource in New England, but Middletown seems not only exploited but ravished. It is a town that gives the immediate impression of having been prosperous some two hundred years ago, when it was the largest town in the state and the principal river port. Perhaps its last energy was drained providing so much of the brownstone that went into the building of nineteenth-century New York City. The only place I could find to moor the launch was a row of slimy, rotten pilings by a small shoreside park, full of litter. I walked through a long underpass beneath an expressway and then through streets lined with shabby convalescent homes, rundown stores, and municipal offices surrounded by acres of parking lot. In the wide otherwise refreshing main street I entered a luncheonette and ordered—dread mistake!—a BLT. After a few minutes I was presented with a scrap of wilted lettuce, three slices of white tomato, and two fragments of bacon, tentatively pressed between pieces of mummified Wonderbread. There was no mayonnaise. The iced coffee was tepid and the only ice cream in stock was chocolate, my least favorite of the twenty-eight flavors. It was a culinary experience that would have colored my view of any town, and Middletown went black. I bought some supplies in an A & P to restock the *Billy Ruffian,* dashed back to the launch, and barreled off down river. Just north of Higganum, a rigorous chop formed where wind and tide met the current. I hugged the eastern shore and hoped no rocks would appear through the quarter-inch skin of the launch.

That night I sat reading by kerosene light, appreciative of my solitude. I had built bunks that were narrow enough to make comfortable seats. Their back boards could be taken down and slotted in to widen the bunk for sleeping on at night. Two Pullman nets held clothes and foul weather gear high out of the way under the foredeck. The kerosene lights lit up the shelves, built between the thick frames, and displayed the jars and canisters on them, the sewing kit, the radio, tools, Conrad's *Nostromo,* charts, and an electric lantern. Aluminum dishes that had held frozen pies formed reflectors for the lights, and two sooty patches on the underside of the deck gave me cause to note that I should buy some more pies, so that I would have the materials to make smoke deflectors over the lights. A job to be done at home.

The week was nearly over, but there was this to be said about cruising in early summer—back in Stonington there were the late afternoons and weekends of all the rest of the season to come. A different but no less pleasurable kind of sailing. Picnic excursions to Sandy Point, with the newest baby, less than a month old, in her swinging basket in the cuddy, slightly older infants sitting happily in the gallon or so of bilge water that collects in a lee corner of the cockpit sole, together with hunks of biscuit, sandy sneakers, and a recently spilled can of ginger ale; Anny pretending to fish with the main sheet; and Liz on the foredeck looking for lobster pot buoys that we might run down.

Tuesday: Downriver in the dory.

7:30 a.m. Up and about. Clear sky. Light airs. Nice morning.

8:30 a.m. Underway with the ebb tide.

10:30 a.m. Picked up a mooring at Essex, then rowed the dinghy into the dock to refill the fuel cans. It was flat calm and hot. Passing the flats of Goose Island I looked across to take a mental snapshot, wondering if I should see the place again and whether it would be the same.

11:30 a.m. Passed through the opened railroad bridge, still with the strong ebb tide, and with the outboard running uncharacteristically well. There were dredges and barges deepening the channel. A breeze now from the southwest, a new feeling. It struck me that rivers provide a different arrangement of reality: calm, warm, withdrawn and even-flowing. At Lynde Point off Saybrook the waters merged, brown in blue. The breeze came from the west in salty gusts, and the *Billy Ruffian* loped into the swell, wetting her dusty sides in the sea.

Appendix A

Dimensions of the Dory Yacht *Billy Ruffian*

length	27 feet 10 inches
breadth	8 feet 4 inches
draft	1 foot 9 inches
draft	4 feet 3 inches (board down)
ballast	500 pounds
approximate sail area	250 square feet

Cost for the first season

hull	$850
spars	18
recutting of sails	35
paint and lumber	85
outboard	25
hoops, hardware, line	14
anchor	12
	$1039

Appendix B

I wish to thank the librarian of the Admiralty Library for this extract from *The Late War between the United States and Great Britain, from June, 1812, to February, 1815. Written in the Ancient Historical Style* by Gilbert J. Hunt (New York: Daniel D. Smith, 1819).

"Chap. XLIII   Attack on Stonington, by the British ships of war which are defeated and driven off.

1. In those days the strong powers of Britain strove hard to quench the fire of Columbian Liberty.
2. But it was lighted up by the hand of heaven, and not to be extinguished.
3. Now it came to pass, on the ninth day of the eighth month of the same year.
4. That the mighty ships of Britain came and opened their thundering engines upon the little town of Stonington, which lieth in the state of Connecticut, in the east.

5. But the inhabitants of the place were bold and valiant men, and they scorned to make a covenant with the servants of the king.

6. Although Hardy, the chief captain of the king's ships had threatened to destroy the place; saying, Remove from the town your women and your children, who are innocent and fight not.

7. Thus shewing more righteousness than any of the king's captains: albeit, he gave them only the space of one hour to depart:

8. So the men of Columbia let the destroying engines loose upon the vessels, and shot the yankee balls amongst them plentifully, and compelled them to depart;

9. Notwithstanding, they had but two of the destroying engines in the place.

10. However, on the eleventh day of the same month, they were again forced to put them in motion.

11. For, in the meantime, Hardy had sent a messenger to the inhabitants, saying,

12. If ye will not prove wicked, and will refrain from sending your evil torpedoes amongst our vessels, then we will
spare your town.

13. Now Hardy was mightily afraid of these torpedoes, (the
history whereof is written in the fiftieth book of these
chronicles) and he trembled at the sound of the name
thereof.

14. Nevertheless, the people of Stonington refused his re-
quest.

15. So the ships of Britain came again and they brought
another strong ship of the king to help them to take the
place.

16. But once more the valiant sons of Connecticut made
them fly for safety: and they came not again.

17. And the gallant conduct of the people of Stonington
gained them much praise, even from the great Sanhedrin
of the people.

18. Thus would the men of Columbia have done, in many
other places, but for the false words and wickedness of
traitorous men.

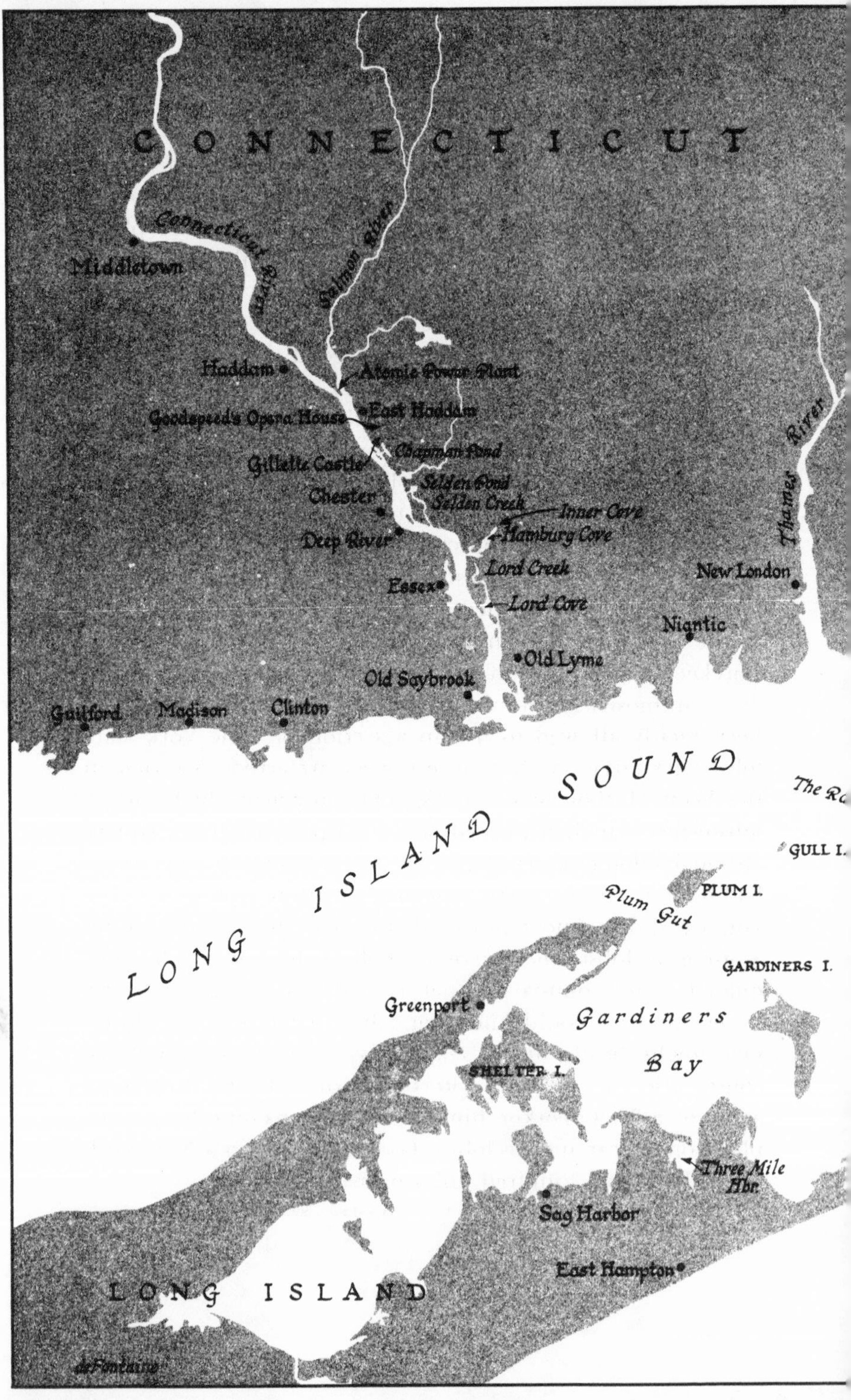

CONNECTICUT
Connecticut River
Salmon River
Middletown
Haddam
Atomic Power Plant
East Haddam
Goodspeed's Opera House
Chapman Pond
Gillette Castle
Selden Pond
Selden Creek
Chester
Inner Cove
Hamburg Cove
Deep River
Lord Creek
Essex
Lord Cove
Thames River
New London
Niantic
Old Lyme
Old Saybrook
Guilford
Madison
Clinton
LONG ISLAND SOUND
GULL I.
PLUM I.
Plum Gut
GARDINERS I.
Greenport
Gardiners Bay
SHELTER I.
Three Mile Hbr.
Sag Harbor
East Hampton
LONG ISLAND
deFontaine

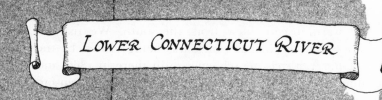

LOWER CONNECTICUT RIVER

Newport •

RHODE ISLAND

•Westerly

Mystic
•
•Stonington

•Watch Hill

Point Judith

BLOCK ISLAND SOUND

ISHERS I.

BLOCK I.

N

Montauk Point

ATLANTIC
OCEAN

0   10   20
              Miles

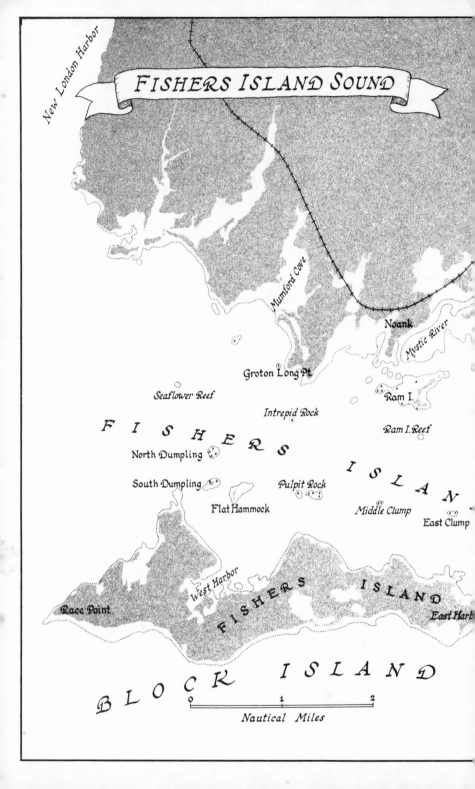

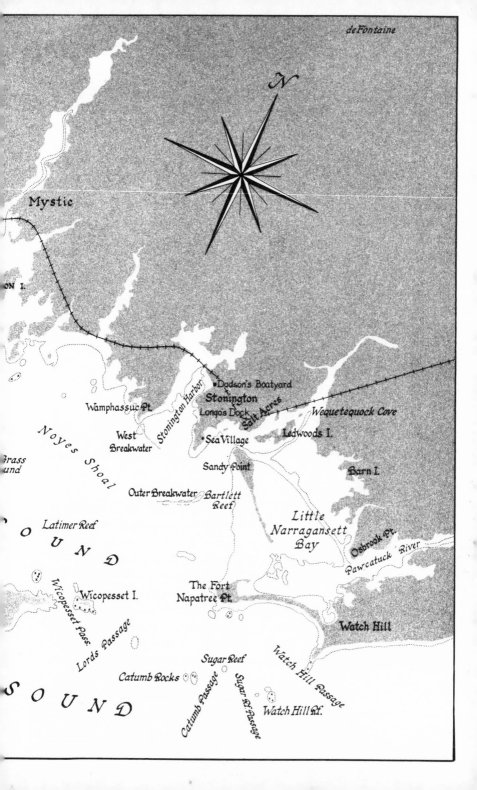

de Fontaine

N

Mystic

ON I.

Dodson's Boatyard
Stonington
Long's Dock   Salt Acres   Weque tequock Cove
Wamphassuc Pt.

West
Breakwater   •Sea Village   Ledwoods I.

Stonington Harbor

Noyes Shoal

Sandy Point

Brass
und   Barn I.

Outer Breakwater *Bartlett
Reef*

*Little
Narragansett
Bay*   Osbrook Pt.

Latimer Reef

Pawcatuck River

Wicopesset I.

Wicopesset Pass

The Fort
Napatree Pt.

Watch Hill Passage

Watch Hill

Lords Passage

Sugar Reef

Catumb Rocks

Catumb Passage   *Sugar Rf. Passage*

Watch Hill Rf.

S O U N D